HANDBOOK OF
CONDUCTING

785.1

HANDBOOK OF
CONDUCTING

By

HERMANN SCHERCHEN

Translated from the German by
M. D. CALVOCORESSI

New Foreword by
NORMAN DEL MAR

OXFORD UNIVERSITY PRESS

Oxford University Press, Walton Street, Oxford OX2 6DP
Oxford New York
Athens Auckland Bangkok Bombay
Calcutta Cape Town Dar es Salaam Delhi
Florence Hong Kong Istanbul Karachi
Kuala Lumpur Madras Madrid Melbourne
Mexico City Nairobi Paris Singapore
Taipei Tokyo Toronto
and associated companies in
Berlin Ibadan

Oxford is a trade mark of Oxford University Press

Published in the United States by
Oxford University Press Inc., New York

© *Oxford University Press 1989*

First published by Oxford University Press in 1933
First paperback edition 1989

British Library Cataloguing in Publication Data
Data available

Library of Congress Cataloging in Publication Data
Scherchen, Hermann, 1891–1966.
[Lehrbuch des Dirigierens. English]
Handbook of conducting | by Hermann Scherchen;
new foreword by Norman Del Mar.
Translation of: Lehrbuch des Dirigiens.
1. Conducting (Music). 2. Orchestral music—Interpretation
(Phrasing, dynamics, etc.) I. Title.
[MT85.S3313 1989] 784.2'145—dc20 89-36992
ISBN 0-19-816182-4

5 7 9 10 8 6 4

Printed in Malta
on acid-free paper by
Interprint Ltd

FOREWORD

My first experience of Hermann Scherchen, that great doyen conductor of contemporary music, was unforgettable. I had been attracted into the large Studio One of the BBC's Maida Vale establishment, normally used for the largest ensembles and especially for the Symphony Orchestra, by strange sounds emanating from within. What I found going on was bewildering: a small chorus assembled to the conductor's left were shouting and screaming, rather than singing, to the sporadic accompaniment of a piccolo, clarinet, and tuba situated centrally, while a heterogenous array of percussion added to the general mêlée. Producers and studio attendants all seemed to be rushing about at the behest of a strange, gnome-like figure with an enormous head, and these frenzied figures included the well-known, and often equally avant-garde conductor Walter Goehr (father of today's distinguished composer and professor, Alexander). A colleague to whom I turned for enlightenment whispered that Scherchen treated Walter Goehr as Walter treated everyone else. The work in rehearsal (for want of a better word) was, I was told, Darius Milhaud's *La Mort d'un Tyran*, which sets an eye-witness account of the mob assassination of the Roman emperor Commodus, a piece the existence of which was known to very few.

The event was wholly typical of the legendary Hermann Scherchen, the author of by far the most absorbing and demanding book on conducting ever published, regular conductor of the pioneering Winterthur Orchestra in Switzerland and whose visits to England never failed to include some wholly unfamiliar and difficult work ('this piece is *very* difficult' were his first words to the London Symphony Orchestra about Hartmann's Eighth Symphony, 'in fact it is *quasi-impossible*'. He it was who had launched the publishing firm Ars Viva in order to make available music by contemporary composers he regarded as scandalously neglected, ranging from Humphrey Searle to Luigi Nono, and whose private life was as unconventional and colourful as his professional exploits. (Married many times, his third and seventh wives were reputed to be one and the same, while in between he always returned to number one. Before childbirth each wife in turn was hastily brought to England so that all his children might have British passports.)

v

FOREWORD

As for Scherchen's *magnum opus*, this *Handbook of Conducting* which has been a veritable Bible for aspiring conductors, it is both utterly visionary and rivetingly interesting. In the first place one wonders what other conductor would, or even could within the space of a few pages, illustrate his points with musical examples taken from Hindemith, Wagner, Beethoven, Strauss, Honegger, Schoenberg, Schumann, Stravinsky, Kaminsky (!), Miaskowsky, Reger, Liszt, Brahms, Mozart, and Bruckner. The very quotations provide for endless and intriguing study. But Scherchen's experience gives the book further value in its deep and far-reaching knowledge of the orchestra itself. I always treasured the fact that in Scherchen's book, alone among all the orchestration manuals, was any mention made of the essential difference between a gong and a tam-tam. His description of a bassoon mute is also fascinating: '... a brass cylinder filling two-thirds of the breadth of the instrument's funnel, six to eight centimetres long, covered with felt, and its outer end stopped with gauze.' Sad to say, such a contraption, which apparently rendered the lower notes to a quality similar to 'the soft notes of a trombone' is wholly unknown today.

Much of the earlier part of the book consists of edicts and strictures, many of which are clearly impracticable in the context of everyday orchestral life as we know it today, sixty years after Scherchen was writing. Musicians themselves have improved immeasurably, both artistically and socially, while the conditions in which they work remain as variable as ever: 'Rehearsals must take place in the concert hall.' Alas, how often is this possible for most orchestras today? 'It is indispensable that the student [of conducting] should play a string instrument well enough to be able to sit in an orchestra.' It would be revealing to know of how many of the world-famous conductors in eminent positions around the world this might now be true. 'It is all-important that wind players should possess, and use, first-class instruments. Let no means be neglected of checking the deplorable custom of using inferior instruments. ... All players of the same instrument should ... have instruments of identical manufacture.' Only an unwise—not to mention intrepid—conductor would make any attempt to confront or criticize his players in this respect when meeting them at the first rehearsal. And so on.

The kernel of the book consists of scrupulously detailed instructions on how to cope with many of the situations encountered during the conductor's journey through an immeasurably wide repertoire. This is dealt with section by section of the orchestra—strings, wind, brass, and percussion, and it is here above all that Scherchen's encyclopaedic knowledge of music is revealed, as well as his ability to select and pinpoint the countless different crises with which the conductor will find himself confronted in the course of his professional activities. In each department he focuses attention on details of style and technique, generally the province of a treatise on instrumentation, but he regards it as pre-eminent that the conductor should be fully in command of these. The profusion of minutiae is extraordinary in a book which is, after all, of no great size.

It is accordingly understandable that the demands of such an uncompromising artist as Scherchen on the conductor, and more still on the student-conductor, are limitless whether in the fields of musicianship, knowledge and understanding of philosophy or, of course, psychology. But if his conception of the ideal conductor is utopian no one can fail to be inspired by such exalted standards as he sets. And if in the closing section of the book Scherchen's edicts on how to conduct various works, bar by bar, gesture by gesture, are didactic to the verge of the absurd ('while the melody ends, the right hand marks time in lingering blunt *staccato* beats, and the eye leads the oboe. With the entry of the first violins the left hand comes in, upbeatwise . . .', etc.), they reveal his experience not only as conductor but as one of the greatest of all teachers of the métier. His book may become old-fashioned in some areas, it may often be pedagogic, it is obviously unrealistic; but paradoxically it will never cease to instruct, to inspire, and above all to enthral rising conductors in the generations to come as it has done so many in the past.

NORMAN DEL MAR

JUNE 1989

PREFACE

By way of Preface I wish to thank Herr Gustav Scheck, the first solo flute of the Königsberg wireless orchestra, who read the proofs of this book with the most painstaking care; my publishers, who by agreeing to the inclusion of hundreds of musical examples, made it possible to substitute practical illustrations for merely theoretic explanations of the problems dealt with; and Herr Neuberg, director of the firm J. J. Weber, for his unremitting attention to the printing and for suggesting many important improvements.

The book is the fruit of my experience acquired during my work at Winterthur, and I must express my gratitude to my friend Werner Reinhart, thanks to whom I was given the opportunity to acquire it, and to the Winterthur Musical Society, whose ready and vigilant co-operation proved stimulating and helpful from beginning to end.

HERMANN SCHERCHEN.

KÖNIGSBERG (PRUSSIA),
JUNE 21, 1929.

CONTENTS

CONTENTS

CONTENTS

ON CONDUCTING

I. THE TEACHABLE TECHNIQUE OF CONDUCTING

IMAGINATION AND REPRODUCTION

The significance of ideal conceptions in music.

THE art of conducting is governed by the fact that the conductor's instrument is a live one, consisting of a number of performers playing a number of different instruments. The conductor's task is to make this complex machine serve the art of music.

As he is playing upon a live instrument, he must understand not only the laws of his art, but also the idiosyncrasies of this instrument; and he will find perforce that he has to form a higher and more spiritual conception of these laws in consequence.

More than any other artist, the conductor must be a master mind, with an imagination capable of conceiving and materializing a musical image. Only when a work has come to absolute perfection within him can he undertake to materialize it by means of the orchestra.

We have to distinguish, then, between the preparatory process, by which the conductor evolves the highest possible ideal conception of a work, and the realization in sounds, the actual conducting (which consists in making things clear to the orchestra and in achieving the performance of the work).

The practice of conducting calls, firstly, for a manual training which is the first step towards acquiring the actual capacity to play on the orchestra. Here, again, the conductor and the orchestra remain apart, and at this stage artistic activity is restricted to a theoretical sphere. To acknowledge that the conductor's domain is largely spiritual is to realize the exceptional character of his art; one can then appreciate the great artistic and human attributes which must be possessed by the true conductor.

Music as the most spiritual of the arts.

The main defect in musical life to-day is lack of imagination on the part of artists. Performers acquire a knowledge of the instrument they play, but never of the works they wish to perform. The technique of the instruments has become an end in itself. The player devotes the whole of his labour to this, but has practically no acquaintance with the technique of composition. And he knows even less of the creative forces.

Music is the most spiritual of arts. Triumph over matter marks the opening of music's greatest era. Werckmeister, when he evolved the tempered semitone system, reduced to order, and subjected to a human, an intellectual law, the unlimited diversity of the materials of music. That which had been sought in vain for nine centuries—the disposal of sounds in proper array, the central form-principle of music—followed, of necessity, upon the new logical hypothesis; the most elusive of materials was captured by the intellect of man.

The secret of art is the secret of personality, whose infinitely various possibilities cannot be counted. But the materials of art can be reckoned up. There is no secret in ordered sound but the secrets of man and of human nature; music proceeds according to human laws, it exhibits an orderliness which is human. Tones and the relations between them can be reckoned up; they have measurable, unequivocally representable values. Good music and good musicians understand one another without aid—without signs indicating dynamics and phrasing, or tempo, expression, and rubato. But that most autocratic of artists, the conductor, is only too often most willing to renounce his power: instead of obtaining his vision of his art from within himself alone, he usually becomes acquainted with musical works through an intermediary. Hence they are obscured by the instrument upon which he plays, and disfigured by the shortcomings of its instrumental technique.

The conductor has to materialize his ideal conceptions.

The conductor, when representing a work to himself, must hear it as perfectly as the creator of this work heard it. A creative artist relies upon the acuteness of his own artistic perception; he hears new tone-colours, he views his materials in a new light, he stamps his own personality upon the music.

Of all the human means of musical expression, singing is the most living or vital. Singing comes from within ourselves. The conductor's conception of a work should be a perfect inward singing. And if the work lives within him as an ideal, undimmed by obstacles of mechanism, then is he worthy to bear the conductor's responsibility. To conduct means to make manifest—without flaws—that which one has perfectly heard within oneself. The sounds must be commanded, and to conduct is to give them shape. The instrument which the conductor uses for this purpose is most sensitive, most richly and diversely equipped and articulated, inexhaustible and most inspiring: it is an organ of which each pipe is a human being. To be able to play this organ is to be a magician; to command it requires almost superhuman powers. But these powers live only in the innermost focus of the ego, at the very source of feeling and inspiration.

The ego must radiate all that it has felt in terms of music; and its radiations must be translated into tones of this magic organ. Only a man who can achieve this mediation in all its purity, in whom are combined the greatest powers of receiving and of giving out again, whose conception of the work does not dwarf it and who is capable of lifting up his medium to the level of that work, is worthy of the name of conductor.

LEARNING HOW TO CONDUCT

Practice before knowledge.

How does one learn to conduct? The current answer is 'By acquiring routine'—which means, by being let loose, without technical knowledge, on works, orchestra, and audience, in order to acquire through 'experience', in the course of long years of anti-artistic barbarity, the tricks of the trade. Apparently there is no other course; one cannot train a conductor as one would a violinist—that is, until he has acquired perfect technique and is fit to appear in public. Of course there is this one saving grace, that an orchestra is a live instrument, comprising sensitive and experienced players who assert their capacity and artistry even in the face of incapacity. For instance, the members of the Berlin Philharmonic orchestra make it a point of honour never to sink beneath a certain level: it is almost harder to obtain from them a really bad performance than to raise their achievements to the highest level.

Whenever the problem is discussed with conductors, one finds them underrating it most presumptuously: 'Conducting cannot be learnt; either one is born a conductor or one never becomes one.' Indeed, there

3

does not even exist a standard method of teaching the technique of our art, a method providing teachers and pupils with materials for systematic exercises and dealing, in a gradual order, with the problems of conducting. All books on conducting published so far contain remarks on practical points, polemics on various conceptions of works, and, at best, advice on how to conduct certain works. Some of them give diagrams showing the principal movements used in conducting. But nothing exhaustive is said about how conducting is achieved or how to learn the art of conducting.[1]

Knowledge before practice.

My intention is to show that a technique of conducting does exist, and can be learnt and practised down to its smallest details before a student first attempts to conduct an orchestra. When the student confronts an orchestra, he must be fully equipped in the matter of technique. He must not be capable only of using with utmost accuracy the processes of his craft, but must know how to subordinate the orchestra's multiple personality to his own conception of the work.

I have trained pupils whom I should be prepared to certify as capable, when facing an orchestra for the first time, of conducting a big orchestral work cleanly and intelligently, *without any rehearsal.* It is at this point that a conductor and an orchestra begin to meet on equal terms, and that any exceptional artistic and musical potentiality in the conductor can be transmitted to the orchestra and find its utterance.

THE STUDENT'S CURRICULUM

Playing in an orchestra.

It is indispensable that the student should play a string instrument well enough to be able to sit in an orchestra. He ought also to learn how to play a wind-instrument, and avail himself of opportunities of playing the percussion. The percussion has steadily been growing more differentiated, and greater specialization is required as

---

[1] There are two signal exceptions: Georg Schünemann's *History of Conducting* and Cahn-Speyer's *Handbook of Conducting.* Both embrace the whole information of which the student stands in need from the historical, aesthetic, and formal points of view; and also, to a certain extent, from the practical. I emphatically recommend that they be used.

4

regards each of the instruments it may include. In music of to-day it often predominates at times, and may even determine the character of a whole movement. It is, then, all the more appalling that many conductors (some of them famous) should be so lacking in experience and imagination in their attitude towards the possibilities of this group.

Studying the instruments.

Some kind of practical study of instrumentation on the lines set by the Berlioz-Strauss treatise is recommended. Let the student apply for help to the principals of each group of instruments, go through works with them, and be thoroughly shown all novel features and all special *virtuoso* effects which each part may include. After the examples given by Berlioz and Strauss, let him study scores by Strauss, Schönberg, Stravinsky, and Hindemith: all these composers set new problems, and set them under a form which has been tested in practical fashion, and proved practicable.

No longer can a conductor face an orchestra with hardly a bare theoretical knowledge of its instruments and their technique. He must have mastered their possibilities with his own hands, and, by virtue of his power of imagination, be capable of animating, stimulating, and offering practical suggestions for the accomplishment of that which is alive within his own imagination.

Choral singing.

To sing in a choir is just as important as to play in an orchestra. Live music always becomes *sung* music, no matter how perfected are the mechanical means by which it is performed. Moreover, the student should learn to conduct a choir: even with the smallest group of singers he will be compelled to learn a certain number of technical devices which he will be able to use when conducting an orchestra: his hands will learn to work independently of one another, and to deal each with certain details.

Full knowledge of works.

The tuition should comprise the most intensive practical study of composition. Side by side with his technical studies, the student should gradually extend his exercises in the technique of composition so as to cover the whole domain of symphonic music. He must learn to determine,

5

in each work, the inner dynamics according to which melody, harmony, rhythm, and architecture are co-ordinated. Only thus will it become possible for him to perceive the constructive principles of each individual work, and deduce from the work itself the correct tempo, style, and technique demanded.

The first condition is that the student should be well grounded in all branches of the science of composition.

EXERCISES FOR DEVELOPING MUSICIANSHIP

Ear.

First of all, the ear should be trained. Let the student sing at sight patterns such as the following. The alpha and omega of all these exercises is that no instrument should be used. The student must learn to hear inwardly what he sees and at once sing (or whistle) it.

Period division according to rhythm and immanent harmony.

Once accuracy of pitch is achieved, the same exercises must be practised in different rhythmic and harmonic conceptions. Thus will the student learn to represent to himself the harmonic relations of the single notes and their values in the bar. The following examples are by way of illustrations, and intended to suggest the invention of other designs.

Three variants of 1 *a.*   Three variants of 1 *b.*

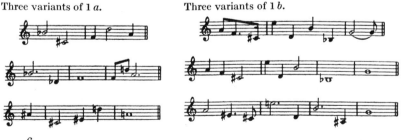

6

Three variants of 1 c.

Melody.

Next, the student should make up melodic patterns—short at first, then gradually longer—of which the first motifs will be dictated to him. He should be taught to determine the centre of gravity, the driving forces, the curving-points of a melody, to master the technique of using these data, and to appreciate the laws of melodic structure.

2

Three variants of 2 *a.*

7

Three variants of 2 *b.*

Three variants of 2 *c.*

Harmony.

After that, the student must learn to realize harmonic formations and their melodic sequence, by regarding certain notes (marked with an asterisk in the examples) as those on which the phrases hinge.

Three variants of 3.

9

Rhythm.

It is essential to develop a very precise, independent sense of metre and rhythm. Let the following exercises be practised systematically (at the uniform tempo ○ = 50).

Division of the unit.

The basis is to be a strictly even step for each unit (○ = step = 50). As he steps, the student will count, without altering the tempo, and without any hurried or retarded transition:

Count	1		1		1	2	1	2	1	2	3	1	2	3
Step														

10

Exercises:

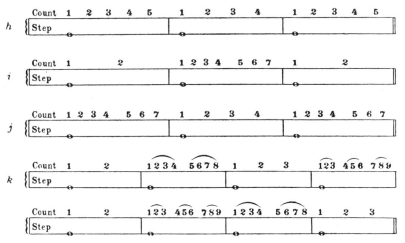

Then let the various metric divisions be combined, the student taking ♩ = 50 as unit and *thinking in units*, but taking two steps to a unit (♪ + ♪ = 100 + 100) and counting:

♩		♩	
one	and	one	and
(step)	(step)	(step)	(step)
= ♪	♪	= ♪	♪

He must always represent to himself the undivided unit as the basis; so that after the

♩		♩	
one	and	one	and
(step)	(step)	(step)	(step)
= ♪	♪	= ♪	♪

has become mechanical enough, he may start counting

Basic unit	♩		♩	
	one	and	one	and
Steps	= ♪	♪	= ♪	♪
	one	two	three	one	two	three
Count	= ♪	♪	♪	= ♪	♪	♪

12

The student will then proceed further according to the following scheme:

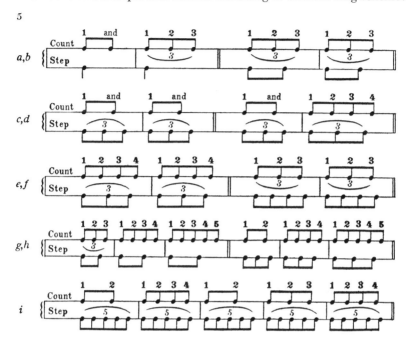

The following exercises are to be performed by the teacher, and repeated from memory by the pupil:

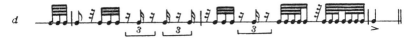

CONDUCTING

Just as the lightning and its flash are one and the same thing, and not two separate things, so, in conducting, the conductor's conception of the work and its materialization in the orchestra must flash forth simultaneously. This absolute unity of conception and sound, of conductor and orchestra, of player and instrument, is the norm which stands before us when we are conducting, is the goal which great conductors, with devoted orchestras, may reach in happy moments.

Orchestra and conductor.

The conductor has three methods of conveying his intentions: representative gesture, expressive mimicry, and explanatory speech. Of these means of establishing an understanding, the first alone interests us. Mimicry and words are of questionable value; they may hamper as well as help. Words, moreover, can be used at rehearsal only.

CLARITY OF CONDUCTING GESTURES

The act of conducting can be defined as follows: gesture, the conductor's one and only medium during performance, must indicate perfectly clearly the metrical course of the work; and at the same time, it must convey in unequivocal fashion the varying expression and general shaping of the work. But the first requirement is that the metrical picture should remain the same and equally clear, whether the motions be large or small, slow or fast, vehement or tender.

14

Mastery over the score.

The pupil must learn the score so thoroughly that during his training he can always conduct from memory. Only then is he free to keep his eyes on the imaginary orchestra. The conductor has nothing to rely on except his personality, and therefore needs the help of his eyes, the chief means of silent communication between human beings. The degree of intimacy of his relations with his players during performance, which in turn depends on his independence of the printed score, will be the measure of his efficiency as a conductor.

How to study.

The pupil's practical work begins at the point where he has acquired full mastery over a portion of the work (be it only ten bars); that is, when he has fixed in his mind and ear its melodic, harmonic, and rhythmic course, the instrumental setting, the prescribed dynamics, and all indications referring to performance. His practice, when he is alone, should be carried out in front of a mirror; for thus he will see himself conducting, and be able to put himself in the place of the performers. Let him form a clear conception of himself as a conductor, react to his own actions, and thus lay the foundation of genuine self-control. The real purpose of the mirror is to warn him against contortions of his body and face. All he does must be natural, simple, unconstrained; and the act of conducting must be accomplished by the right arm only. At lesson-time, it is the teacher who stands as a member of the orchestra, perceiving and watching. The pupil faces him, conducts him, governs him with gestures and eyes.

Ten bars of a masterpiece, learnt by heart, perfectly conceived and interpreted in the most ideal form possible, mean the comprehension and solution of a whole array of problems. And all that has been learnt thereby need only be brought to bear, with suitable variations, upon other music, to prove again serviceable.

The pupil, while conducting, must not only represent the music to himself but actually sing it within himself. The music must ring within him, ideally, and as living expressive sound, so that the movements calling it forth from the orchestra may be entirely spontaneous, a means

15

to an end, but never an end in themselves, mere self-assertion, or useless gesticulation.

Representative gesture and imagined sound.

Let every gesture represent singing tone, summarizing that tone through its various stages of abstract conception, visible interpretation, to audible realization. Let it acquire the smoothness which characterizes perfect instruments; let it be simple, intelligible, quite unambiguous, restricted to a minimum, and yet carrying all the needful meaning. Let it be a lightning-stroke radiating orchestral tone, encompassing, co-ordinating, and permeating all the manifold and wonderfully diverse energies of the orchestra.

II. IDIOSYNCRASIES OF CONDUCTING

REPRESENTATION OF WORKS

THE actual motions of conducting which are described later in the book represent only one individual technique. By mastering these, the pupil will eventually be able to form his own peculiar technique, as he works with his teacher. Various builds of body may lead to various speeds, a greater or smaller length of arm to corresponding differences in the amplitude of movements. All such individually conditioned restrictions or inclinations, without any exception, must be governed by this supreme law: the executive technique of conducting must obey the preconception which the conductor has formed of the work, which preconception determines the technique to be employed and adapts all externals to its own ends.

The ideal preconception.

As executive orchestral technique must be solely subservient to the preconception of the work to be performed, this preconception determines the mode of bowing (or, as regards wind-instruments, of blowing) instead of technical routine determining the preconception of the tone and mode of attack required. In other words, all the physical operations involved in performance must be inspired by the abstract conception of the music.

16

Clarity.

The first condition for the materialization of a musical work is perfect clarity of conception. Failing this, the work remains incomplete. Again, the first condition for clarity is perfect technical correctness in orchestral performance. The first maxim of conducting should read: ill-defined performance and incorrect playing spell misrepresentation.

Unpremeditation.

The ideal musical performance should present the work as coming into existence, without any appearance of deliberation, without effort. The work must seem to materialize of itself. No *crescendo* must appear conscious, no *ritardando* or *rubato* enforced. The performance must be as natural as the process of breathing. The necessary conditions are a thoroughly live preconception and a technically unambiguous materialization.

THE PERFORMER'S STANDARD

The orchestra.

This ideal calls for complete independence on the player's part. This is possible only when each player stands as a brother artist, co-operating in constructive work. The conception of the orchestra as a perfect machine belongs to the past. It gives a false picture of a self-evident, necessary condition.

The level of the orchestra can never be too high: it should never be needful to rehearse elementary things. The more intelligence players bring to bear on their job, the fewer details will the conductor have to bother about. Such things will become a matter of course. More will be said on this problem in the chapters devoted to the orchestra and its functions.

The conductor.

A high level of capacity and training is required of the players, a far higher one is required of the conductor. He is the vehicle for the manifestation of spiritual art. He must be able to interpret great music written in styles ranging over many centuries. In the course of one season, the repertory of works he has to conduct greatly exceeds in

17

number and variety anything that a violinist or pianist has to deal with; and all these works have their own idiosyncrasies of style and contents, of means selected, of form and orchestral garb. Even the specialized experience needful in other arts, such as that of the stage (which calls for the activities not of one but of several producers—of the modern, realistic expert and of the Shakespeare expert), cannot compare with the singularly representative position of the conductor. Therefore it is all the more important to determine the qualifications which will entitle him to hold worthily his high position as an artist.

The basis of his activities should be a thoroughly live general culture. Let us consider the medley of styles of the last decade or so: impressionism, expressionism, individualism, community art, new classicism, new materialism, movement-music, workaday music, twelve-tone music, quarter-tone music—a profusion of various conceptions, and ventures in style, of experiments and solutions, of abstraction and genuine art. Stravinsky cannot be played in the same way as Schönberg, nor Hindemith as Křenek; and the differences between Busoni and Pfitzner, Kaminski and Webern, Honegger and Strauss are not to be ignored.

In every generation, the law governing individuals asserts itself. What is true to-day characterizes every century: thus we have Wagner against Brahms, Bruckner against Reger, Beethoven against Schubert, Mozart against Gluck, Handel against Bach—a profusion of forces each bearing its individual stamp, a wealth of diverse personalities. The conductor must encompass them all, awaken them within himself through his own personality. However extensive the scope of his imaginative powers, his comprehension will remain limited unless he is adequately equipped with knowledge. He must be acquainted with cultural history, and realize the relationship of events in musical history. The former must help him to determine the conditions under which creative personalities acquire their characteristic form. The latter must provide him with the means of disengaging from the idiosyncrasies of a period the idiosyncrasies of the individual. He must be capable of distinguishing between the style of the period and the style of the man, between general conventions and individual conventions. In his art he is the distributor of life, who resurrects or annihilates both individuals and centuries.

Knowledge of philosophy must reveal to him the outlook upon the

18

world which informs an artist's creations. Schopenhauer's world of thought has disclosed provinces of feeling which had previously not found their expression in music. Listen to Wagner's 'Five Poems by Mathilde Wesendonck', in which Schopenhauer's conceptions are transmuted into poetry. Wagner has given them form in music which envisages new regions of human experience. Think of Mozart's 'Magic Flute', of the lofty significance of this childlike play. The pure, deep sublimity of the effect it produces echoes the emotional value, to Mozart and his contemporaries, of the ideals of the new citizenhood as embodied in freemasonry. And how could any one visualize Beethoven's mental strife without knowing anything of the individual problems of Beethoven, torn between the consciousness of his own self and his ideals of brotherhood with his fellow men; between his own creative autocracy and his desire to sink and lose himself in universal humanity; of the endless battle that is apparent in the G major Concerto, that rings in the opening and final cries of the Allegretto of the Seventh Symphony, and finally, after the transport of the insistent 'All men become brothers!' leads the artist, in his loneliness, to hesitate, fear, and ask: 'But will all men become brothers?'

The range of our prescriptions becomes greater and greater. Let it be repeated that the conductor's activities are exclusively spiritual; that the spirit is the mightiest human power; and that we had to define the conductor as the most spiritual form of the manifestation of reproductive art. No man is adequate to so lofty a calling unless the spiritual really lives within him, and encompassing knowledge is associated with sensitiveness and creative organization.

THE PROBLEMS OF CONDUCTING

Intuition and critical watchfulness.

The peculiarity of the conductor's task is that it requires both intuitive organization and critical watchfulness. His gestures fulfil a two-fold function: they have to present the work and to guide the players. This means that he must watch and correct, prepare and simplify, adjust mistakes in the course of the execution, prevent and counteract wrong developments. He is, so to speak, the watchful conscience of the orchestra: he observes, supports, and assists. It is only when perfect mastery over a work enables him freely to fulfil all these functions that performance really runs smoothly. The gestures must outline both the rhythmic structure of the work and the presentment of its expressive and constructional features. Thirdly, they should give shape to the performance, determining its quality and raising it to the highest possible level.

The teacher as practice-orchestra.

The teacher has to train the pupil not only in presenting the work, but in overcoming the difficulties inherent to practice. The pupil's gestures, besides providing an unequivocal expression of the work, must acquire the power of handling the orchestra with sovereign authority. To this effect, the teacher, when following the pupil's guidance, must assume various demeanours:

(1) That of an exemplarily sensitive orchestra, which follows every movement of the conductor perfectly; this will provide a corrective to exaggeration, because under such conditions every excess of gesture results in excess of effect.

(2) That of an orchestra of medium quality, which is willing to react but needs stimulus—in which case the conductor at times must help, e.g. in progressions and in the matter of their correct development, in changes of tempo, shades of expression, in balancing tonal volumes, &c.

(3) That of a bad and uninterested orchestra, to govern which all that the conductor does spontaneously proves insufficient—in which case there is no longer any distinction between gestures whose object is to represent the music and gestures whose end is the practical purpose of guiding and urging the musicians; the conductor's will-power stands on the same plane as his intuitive vitalization of the work.

THE EXECUTANTS' RESPONSIBILITY

Music lives only when actually heard: the fleeting tones are the only reality which musical works possess. It is not possible to correct mistakes in music except by preventative diagnosis. A mistake overlooked becomes part and parcel of a work. Tuition, therefore, must develop presence of mind, a capacity to anticipate and control. Faulty, uneven, feeble things in performance must be foreseen by the conductor and staved off.

Until now it was admitted that this essential part of the art of conducting could only be learnt by dint of long practice in actual performance. With this most inartistic notion was associated, most amusingly, the notion of a kind of divine grace, which comfortably ticked off conducting as a gift from Heaven: 'Conducting cannot be taught. One is either born a conductor or one never learns to become one.' The force of personality and artistic potency cannot be acquired; that much is nature's gift. Moreover, there are certain particular initial conditions which predestine certain human beings to be singers, others to be instrumentalists, others to be conductors. But all professional training is of a technical order; and the technique of conducting must be learnt, as any other. When conductors try to learn their job from an orchestra the orchestra should refuse to play. A virtuoso instrumentalist performing works of art without having acquired adequate technical grounding is an impossibility; but an exactly analogous situation has arisen in the course of all conductors' education and actual career even up to the present day.

III. ORCHESTRAL PLAYING AND CONDUCTING

THE ORCHESTRA'S IDIOSYNCRASIES

The sounds of the orchestra.

THIS book does not deal with questions of conception and interpretation. These belong to the study of music itself, which study governs all performance. The remarks that follow are specially connected with the problem of conducting.

A note when actually sounding may vary in pitch, loudness, duration, volume, colour, character, intensity, and production, according to the mode of attack. All these particularities are inseparable, even if we restrict them to a minimum, and are always present (e.g. in the sounds emitted by a violin, a voice, a piano). But orchestral sound is even more diverse. The orchestra not only includes all the instruments, but associates together various groups of instruments. Take for instance the

A of the once-accented octave, and apportion it to various instruments thus:

The degree of loudness will remain apparently unaltered. The *mf decrescendo pp* of the horn is balanced by a contrasting *pp crescendo mf* of the oboe; but the *mf* of the oboe is different from that of the horn, so that the result is a slight *decrescendo*. Its duration will be imperceptibly reduced by the *tremolo* of the violins, which at the climax introduces changes of loudness, volume, and colour. The volume of this A, as started by the flute and horn, is appreciably greater than the volume provided at the end by the flute and oboe. The colour, on the contrary, has changed from a soft and dark one to a clearer one; the *dolce* of the beginning with the flute and horn has acquired, through the oboe, the character of a neutral *mf*, and the intensity of the note has appreciably increased. In other words, the note has remained the same, but its properties have changed; while loudness and volume decreased, colour, character, and intensity were increasing.

Orchestral execution.

This brings us up against an art-phenomenon which has a special significance as regards the playing of the orchestra. We have seen that in any one note, alterations or exchanges of separate properties can take place. Far more significant in practical performance is the fact that tempo, loudness, mode of performance, rhythm, energy, tone-production, and tone-quality can replace and enhance one another.

The common measure between them is the inner intensity predetermining their application. We must make a distinction between direct intensity (the strength and reinforcement of separate factors), and indirect intensity (sudden weakening and fading out of the factors), which is made manifest as suspense, slowing down, or unresolved tension. Cases in point are:

(1) The first violins, wandering upwards and fading away before the big outburst in the Funeral March in the 'Eroica':

8 Beethoven: 'Marcia funebre' of IIIrd Symphony

(2) In the C minor Symphony, the resolution into *pizzicato* of the Scherzo theme just before the transition to the Finale:

9 Beethoven: 3rd Movement of Vth Symphony

(3) The following bars in which the melody climbs higher and higher above the C of the timpani as a preparation for the eight bars of *crescendo* transition to this Finale:[1]

10 Beethoven: 3rd Movement of Vth Symphony

[1] Here we are reaching provinces of musical composition which have not yet been investigated deeply enough. Let us take two important particular cases:

(1) The significance of the breaking up of a theme as practised by Beethoven at the end of the slow movements of the 'Eroica' and of the 'Coriolan' Overture:

(*Note 1 continued on p. 24.*)

INTENSIFICATION

Intensity, physical and psychical.

It is an established law that increased psychical energy tends to show itself in the form of increased physical energy. Physical energy is anti-musical: music, the art of the spirit and of spiritual tensions, cannot endure physical energy as an end in itself.

(*Note* 1 *continued from p.* 23.)

11 Beethoven: 'Marcia funebre' of IIIrd Symphony

12 Beethoven: Overture 'Coriolan'

(2) The driving power of changing pitch and its power to act as a brake:

(*a*) When steadily upward, by way of preparation and *crescendo*-effect (particularly powerful in the transitional rise before the Finale of the C minor Symphony, in which the tension of the progress upwards is so much increased by the impeding effect of the uniform *pp* as to become almost unendurable (see Ex. 10)).

(*b*) The wandering from instrument to instrument, and the sinking to the depths in the last bars of the Allegretto of the VIIth Symphony:

13 Beethoven: Allegretto of VIIth Symphony

24

To allow inner intensity to slacken while loudness, tempo, and rhythm remain unaltered results in enfeebling these factors. A way of applying the above law would be to build up a *crescendo* approximately according to the following plan:

Suppose that the strings carry out the whole of a *crescendo*, that woodwinds come in gradually, and that shortly before the climax the brass and percussion reinforce the last stages. The woodwinds, as they come in gradually, should begin by playing *piano* without *crescendo*: the very fact that more instruments are playing produces a distinct *crescendo* effect. Then, at the moment when the strings arrive at the *forte*, let the pace of their *crescendo* be retarded, and the woodwinds gradually rise from *piano* to *forte* while the strings rise from *forte* to *fortissimo*. At this point, let resources be husbanded afresh: while the woodwinds rise from *forte* to *fortissimo* the brass should be brought from *piano* to *forte*. For the percussion, the rate of progress should be only half as quick, so that by the time all the other instruments are playing *fortissimo*, the percussion should be playing *mezzo forte*, reserving its final *crescendo* for the very apex, when all the other instruments, having reached the maximum of their physical power, bring in, in addition, increased energy of rhythm, of accent, and of melodic motion—in short, a general *crescendo* of psychical intensity.

Combination of various factors.

While this gradation is being effected dynamically, there is another way of building it up: by combining various factors. One may use, to this effect:

The passing from *legato* to *staccato*:

14   Schubert: 1st Movement of B minor Symphony

25

The tempo remains the same, but the rhythmic values are shortened:

15   Honegger: 'Pacific 231'

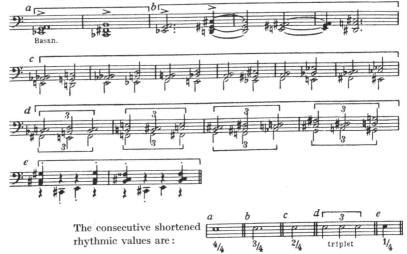

The consecutive shortened
rhythmic values are:

$^4/_4$ $^3/_4$ $^2/_4$ triplet $^1/_4$

Repetitions of irregular patterns (six then seven quavers) in a long, metrically uniform impetus:

16   Beethoven: IIIrd Leonore Overture

p e sempre cre - - - - - scen - - -

- do - - - - - - - - -

Gradual rise of melodic arabesques:

17   Beethoven: 4th Movement of VIIth Symphony

sempre più *f*

26

Repetition with increasing energy of motifs pressing forwards.

18   Strauss: 'Till Eulenspiegel'

Honegger's study in *crescendo*, 'Pacific 231', is a model as regards association of the most diverse factors. The problem, in this work, was to convey the illusion of ceaselessly increasing speed and display of power, without resorting to alteration of the basic tempo. A thorough study of this stroke of genius will make the student acquainted with a quantity of apposite solutions of this problem.

LIMITATION AN ENRICHMENT

Music without shades of expression. Metre and rhythm.

′ A remarkable phenomenon of our time is the coming of Stravinsky, whose art altogether repudiates certain factors of music. In his latest works there is neither a *crescendo* nor a *diminuendo*. All that is expressive motion in the build of melody (i.e. *accelerando, ritardando,* or *rubato* for expressive purposes) is excluded. All romantic expressive adjuncts being ignored, the music has to rely on its own intrinsic power exclusively, on its manifold, stimulating, strictly set-out course and its arrangement into terse patterns. This art obeys a different law of organization from that which governs both classical and modern music. The rhythms and thematic materials of the work go their way over a most strictly partitioned and jointed framework of metre, whose level is most carefully calculated and whose parts are most nicely interadjusted. The contrast

27

between the strict form-building metric scheme and the motley wealth of the rhythmic course produce a new kind of tension, which replaces the usual expressive tensions.

19   Stravinsky: 'Les Noces'

This music needs the help of an instrument used very restrictedly in other music: here the *metronome* plays a decisive part; time has to be carefully measured, and its divisions accurately correlated.

Let us consider 'Noces' (1916—a Cantata for choir, 4 solo voices, 4 pianos, and 6 percussion players). Throughout the work we have 240 as smallest measure-unit. The first tempo, $\eighth = 80$, contains this unit as part of a triplet. The second tempo, $\eighth = 160$, is twice as fast, and its relation to the unit is that of 2 to 3. The third tempo, $\quarter = 80$, contains the unit as the value of the quaver in the triplet. In the next tempo, $\quarter = 120$, which is the main tempo of the whole work, the unit corresponds exactly to the quaver. So that we have the following metric relationships:

$$\quarter = 80, \text{ or } 1:3$$
$$\eighth = 160, \text{ or } 2:3$$
$$\dottedquarter = 80, \text{ or } 1:3$$
$$\quarter = 120, \text{ or } 1:2$$

This intentionally impoverished music exploits an extraordinary variety of rhythms. Its big stretches of *forte* and *piano*, unconnected by any expression-*crescendo*, require a most accurate performance in which no single stroke of the design is blurred. The idiosyncrasies of the presentment of such works, from the point of view of conducting technique, will be discussed further.

SONG THE BASIC LAW OF ALL MUSICAL REPRODUCTION

The piano.

The piano as the instrument used in the home has acted on music as a plague, and wrought terrible havoc. Even in orchestras, people are to be encountered whose musical training has taught them to decompose all melodic relationships into small parts. Just as the guileless pianist conceives a bass which merely signifies a harmonic displacement as a division of structural articulation, so do other players hack periods in 4/4 into half-bars, and partition live melodic entities into metric fragments. For instance, one often hears the following two melodies played as I write them down (the actual signatures are 4/4 and 2/2 respectively):

20 *a*   Wagner: Rienzi Overture

b   Weber: Freischütz Overture

Now what is it that is wrong, what is it that causes such well-built rhythmic designs to be divided into meaningless half-bar caricatures?

Singing.

German players are subject to a hereditary evil: they do not or cannot sing enough. Often we conductors encounter orchestral playing in which all possible virtues—accuracy, elasticity, evenness, power, &c.— are united, but in which we miss one thing: the soul of music, the song that gives inward life to musical sounds.

To sing is the life-function of music. Where there is no singing, the forms of music become distorted and they move in a senseless time-order imposed from without.

Two kinds of crescendo.

To inhale is to concentrate, to exhale is to release. Thus, all singing is concentration and release. Every melody carries its form-giving motion up to a central point, from which point onwards the notes are released. Concentration is tension; tension seems to be *crescendo*; and *crescendo*, conversely, is the music's urge to reach its central point.

This tension-*crescendo* must be sharply differentiated from the expression-*crescendo* of the post-classical composers. It is not our business to investigate whether the latter was invented by the Italian or the

Mannheim school. One thing is sure: that the composers of the Mannheim school excelled in it; Mozart learnt it from them, and Beethoven adopted their technique.

To this school belongs the singular merit of having been the first to cultivate for its own sake that most extraneous property of tone, its volume, using it in rising and falling gradations. Later, the pseudo-psychological evolution of music found therein an important resource: recourse to dynamic values superseded invention; the great earthquake in Mahler's 'Resurrection' Symphony (the Second Symphony) consists of mere dynamic noise, of an inarticulate *crescendo* of the percussion. But the technique of phrasing provides us with the means which, rightly applied, will produce the effect of the tension-*crescendo*. Here we hardly have to deal at all with a real increase in the loudness of the tone: rather with a straining of the sounds towards their goal, which only creates the illusion of a *crescendo*.

Crescendo of intensity.

Let us take the 'Freischütz' example. The harmonic motion is effected in the fourth bar. In the first three, the E flat major chord rises in a melodic pattern consisting of turns and of real notes; and then— when the dominant harmony has entered—sinks, with the suspension C–B flat, back to its starting-point. The motion of these three bars is like a drawing in of breath, and tends straight to the suspension, which has an important significance, relaxing the effort, the tension, and starting the second, answering, waning, part of the phrase.

21 *a* Weber: Freischütz Overture

b Wagner: Rienzi Overture

In the 'Rienzi' example, in which we have the cadence I–V⁶–IV–I⁶, a natural melodic *crescendo* takes place simultaneously with the forward

---

[1] The author uses the sign ———➤ to denote a *crescendo* of intensity.

30

motion of the harmony, and is emphasized by the upward swing of the turn. Both examples show the tension-*crescendo*: in the one from 'Freischütz' owing to the motion, in that from 'Rienzi' actually perceptible as an increase in loudness owing to the intensive urge of the harmonic movement.

Expression-crescendo.

A pregnant example of expression-*crescendo* is found in the beginning of the 'Tristan' Prelude.

22 Wagner: Tristan Prelude

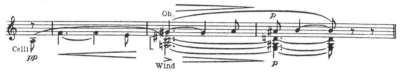

The dynamics (accurately prescribed by the composer) are justified and rendered necessary by the psychological parallelism of painful yearning and of confused and weary dropping back. There is a similar expression-*crescendo* in the first movement of Tchaikovsky's Pathetic Symphony.

23 Tchaikovsky: 1st Movement of VIth Symphony

Singing, the life-function of music.

Singing not only is the primary condition of correct melody-moulding, but sets the pace at which the melody should go (see Wagner's *On Conducting*, in which the main features of a study of tempo are considered from a general point of view). Italian and French instrumentalists play in terms of singing, but the German, as a rule, in strictly instrumental terms; that is, instead of subordinating their technique to the requirements of singing, they impede the flow of singing with their technical routine. Technical routine and metrically divided piano-playing are evils which falsify and obstruct the very essence of music: all music both in conception and in actualization is singing.

31

THE SCIENCE OF THE ORCHESTRA

I. THE BOW INSTRUMENTS

THE LEADER AND HIS DUTIES

Conception and technique.

WE have blamed the German instrumentalist for his incapacity to play in terms of singing, and established a general law for musical performance: preconception must never be subordinated to technique. This law sums up all that conductor and orchestra have to achieve: its fulfilment in an artistically flawless interpretation is the ideal of musical performance.

The leader, in bygone times the conductor's rival, must be nowadays his main helper. A leader in whom sound musicianship, interest in art, and general culture are combined with virtuosity, experience in chamber-music, and a capacity for efficient leading, may exercise an invaluable function; he may ennoble and influence the tone of the whole orchestra.

The conductor's adjutant.

The conductor must be able fully to depend upon him and entrust him with all indirect problems concerning conducting. Among these problems are:

(a) *Tuning-in.*

This should take place, not on the platform, but before the players enter. Let a tuning-fork be placed in the tuning-room, and the wind take their pitch from it with the utmost care.

Wind.

One trusted member of the woodwind group and one of the brass should make sure that all instruments of the same group have tuned-in with one another, including a careful adjustment of the pitch of identical instruments. It is particularly important that clarinets and flutes should be perfectly attuned. The same applies to the trumpets and trombones. But both wind groups should pay the utmost attention to keeping in tune with one another.

Bow instruments.

These must be verified by the leader, who, before each goes on to the platform, should once again listen to their A. Loud tuning-up should be absolutely forbidden. The A of the oboe, as often as not, will be incorrectly taken over; for as soon as it is heard, all the string players start running *fortissimo* over all the strings of their instruments and drown it.

In order to ensure as durable a pitch as possible, all instruments should be well played twenty minutes before the concert starts, and all players should be on the platform at least ten minutes before starting-time. The temperature of the hall must have no further effect on the pitch during the concert; and with this object, the instruments must have adjusted themselves to it in good time.

Absolute silence must reign on the platform. Necessary corrections of pitch must be carried out *pp*. A concert is an event which should be informed with a certain solemnity. A decorous attitude on the orchestra's part contributes to this end.

Percussion.

The principal of the percussion group should take care that the instruments whose notes are indeterminate should remain true to character: the triangle, cymbals, tamtam, and bells should produce no determinative overtones.

The case is different, however, when several kinds of drums have to give out differentiated notes, and also with regard to bells, cymbals, and tamtam. A good timpanist, with a sense of his responsibility, will see to it that the right instruments are available, that 'deep' bells should not create an impression of high clear tones, that small cymbals should not sound as dull as kettle-lids, that a big tamtam should really give forth a heavy, sombre boom. Above all, the pitch of the timpani should be adjusted with the utmost care. Special effects aimed at by composers should come off quite clearly if the performance is flawless. A case in point is the trill of the violas on the A which comes as a resolution, in a brighter colour, of the timpani's *tremolando* on B flat in Strauss's 'Till Eulenspiegel'.

33

24 Strauss: 'Till Eulenspiegel'

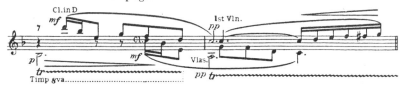

Controlling the pitch.

It is the leader who exercises the supreme control over the correctness of the orchestra's pitch. He finally ensures that all three groups of instruments which give out definite notes should be well attuned to one another.

(b) Collocation of the orchestra.

First and second violins.

It is to be recommended that the violins' desks should not stand parallel with the sides of the conductor's desk; because, if so, the players sitting nearest to the audience will be looking away from the conductor and into the depths of the orchestra. Far better place the desks obliquely, so that the conductor will stand well within every player's field of vision.

The question of space and light.

The orchestra must have sufficient space for players never to cramp one another; every desk must have adequate light, and from all, the conductor must be easily and clearly seen.

There must be an adequate contact between those players in every group who belong together. This rule applies not only to the woodwind and brass, but to the percussion, whose accuracy may suffer through bad collocation.

(c) Rehearsing accommodation.

The ideal place for rehearsing is the concert hall itself.

Rehearsals must take place in the concert hall. Any other acoustic conditions will induce new relationships of tones. In a smaller space, things which in the concert hall would come off *f* or *p dolce* may sound overloud or rough.

34

The first condition is that rehearsals should take place under comfortable conditions. The musicians should not have to sit in an unheated hall. Let these remarks not be considered as pedantic: the conductor's work is carried out with conscious human beings. Every needless discomfort means waste of precious time.

The leader and the representative of the players.

Let us revert to the leader. He, the conductor's confidential deputy, in co-operation with one member of the orchestra selected as all the players' confidential deputy, should regulate all such matters which do not directly concern the conducting.

Second Violins, Violas, Basses—principal or accessory parts?

It is essential that all parts of the string-orchestra should be equally well filled. The second violins, the violas, the double-basses should not be entrusted to inferior players. At auditions for selection, no distinction should be drawn: the second violins and violas have the same duties to perform as the first violins.

IDIOSYNCRASIES OF BOW-INSTRUMENT TECHNIQUE

(*a*) FINGER- AND BOW-ACCENT

The accent made by means of the bow is used for direct accentuation; the accent made by means of the finger serves the purpose of emphasizing the articulation.

The accent made with the finger is used as follows:

To emphasize the articulation.

(1) When there is no need for an actual accent, but the clearness and intensity of the attack must be stressed:

25   Wagner: Meistersinger Overture

26   Mozart: 4th Movement of Jupiter Symphony

27   Bruckner: 2nd Movement of IXth Symphony

To replace the bow-accent.

(2) Instead of the bow-accent in a *pianissimo*:

28   Weber: Euryanthe Overture

The accent made with the bow is used:

To start a motif.

(1) When the beginning of a motif has to be sharply marked:

29   Beethoven: 4th Movement of Vth Symphony

Delineation.

(2) In order to outline a pattern:

30   Beethoven: Eroica, 1st Movement

Marking the main notes of the harmony.

(3) In order to bring out the main notes of chords broken up into figured patterns:

31   Weber: Euryanthe Overture

Bringing out motifs.

(4) In order clearly to mark divisions between sectional motifs:

32   Weber: Oberon Overture

Accentuating syncopations.

(5) To sharpen the forward impetus of syncopated notes:

33   Weber: Freischütz Overture

fp *accent.*

The bow-accent may occur as *fp* under three forms:

(6) To bring out expressively accented notes (genuine *fp*):

34   Beethoven: Pastoral Symphony, 2nd Movement

fp decrescendo.

(7) As an abbreviation for *f decrescendo p*:

35   Mozart: Jupiter Symphony, 2nd Movement

fp *caesura.*

(8) To show that an impetus has reached its goal:

36   Strauss: 'Till Eulenspiegel'

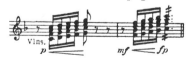

(b) LEGATO

The following methods of *legato* tone production must be accurately differentiated:

'Harmonic' stroke.

(1) The slow, silky stroke of the whole length of the bow (similar to the stroke used to produce harmonics), introduced into the orchestra by Mahler.

37 Mahler: 2nd part of VIIIth Symphony

Bow drawn pp.

(2) The *pp* singing tone produced by the use of the light whole bow, drawn gently without insistent friction:

38 Mahler: 2nd Movement of IIIrd Symphony

Gliding, non espressivo pp.

(3) The numb *pp* tone produced by the bow resting on the strings almost motionless, gliding to its end slowly without pressing or drawing:

39 Busoni: Dead March (No. 8) from 'Turandot'

Legato *figuration.*

(4) The quietly drawn bow *pp* in figured melodies:

40 Beethoven: 1st Movement of IXth Symphony

Uniformly smooth singing stroke.

(5) The uniformly gliding, singing stroke:

41   Beethoven: Violin Concerto, 1st Movement

ff legato '*stroke by stroke*'.

(6) The *legato* in *fortissimo* strokes, which, by virtue of the mellowness of the stroke and the drawing of the whole bow, must maintain throughout the slurred character:

42   Weber: Euryanthe Overture

pp espressivo.

(7) The drawn *pp espressivo*:

43   Busoni: March (No. 4) from 'Turandot'

The perfect legato.

Drawing, stroking, gliding.

The necessary condition of a perfect *legato* is that the three possible ways of achieving *legato*-singing tone (drawing, stroking, gliding) should never be mixed; that downbow drawing should not be followed by upbow stroking, and also that the actual duration of the up- and downbow movements should be carefully calculated, and in many cases remain the same.

39

44   Beethoven: 3rd Movement of IXth Symphony
(A way in which it often is performed.)

| DRAWN downbow, beginning with a wrong pressure by the nut; it gradually tends to a duller tone, as the bow is allowed to GLIDE. | Quick upbow STROK-ING, resulting in a wrong *crescendo*, emphasizing the E, and tonelessly running through the demisemiquavers (but see footnote [1]). |

Sources of mistakes.

When a melody continues quietly rising and falling, and suggests an absolute equality between inhalation and exhalation, there is a danger that in performance it will be cut up into short-winded little patterns, giving an asthmatic caricature thus:

Equal distribution of bowing.

Let this passage be played with an absolutely equal distribution of the drawn bow (one-third of the total length to each quaver), and its natural phrasing result from the weight of the stroke:

— + = Barely perceptible tension-*crescendo*.

The tone-quality of a *legato* depends entirely upon the action of the left hand:

Intensive slow legato *singing tone*, pp.

(1) Its intensity may carry the restful tone of the luxuriously slow *pp* singing in the final *Adagio* of Mahler's Third Symphony to the highest

[1] Of course all this is overstated. But as the comments refer to faults that are always cropping up, the exaggeration may be allowed to pass.

degree of vitality, if the fingers move to each single note of the melody with an almost tender pressure (see Ex. 38).

Animating accompaniment patterns.

(2) Likewise, the following *pp* gliding *Allegro* design—

47   Weber: Freischütz Overture

may be given animation by a light *vibrato*-pressure of the left hand. Unless the left hand aims at holding each single note in it with caressing tenderness, the design will sound dull and exercise-like. Here we are dealing with an important resource in the matter of melody-building. Passages which for the most various reasons do not sound well can be made to sing, and be elucidated and dematerialized, by over-expanding, hammering, or lightening various subdivisions of them.

Over-expanding.

(3) (*a*) The following example shows the use of over-expansion:

48   Beethoven: Great Fugue, Op. 133

(*b*) Let the 'celli and double-basses play the following passage not only *ff*, but also with the determination to sustain each note intensively, and (while keeping strict tempo) almost over-expanding each demisemi-quaver. None of the usual readjustments will then be needed to ensure that the melodic pattern will be heard clearly.

49   Beethoven: 2nd Movement of Vth Symphony

Hammering.

(4) (*a*) The following passage embodies, in the melodic run of the ascending scales, the storming of the upper octave. When playing it,

41

let the fingers of the left hand hit the string like a hammer, achieving very quick finger-accents. The *legato* character being well maintained, the ascending passage will be endowed with the requisite growing intensity.

50   Beethoven: 2nd Movement of Vth Symphony

(*b*) Example 51 contains small connecting notes which must be distinctly heard. They must be 'hammered' in the same way.

51   Mozart: 4th Movement of Jupiter Symphony

'*Lightening.*'

(5) (*a*) The object of 'lightening' is to reduce melodic consistence to a minimum. It may be used in *Adagio* as well as in *Allegro*. The fingers must barely lay hold of each note and pass on, gently and without pressure, to the next (see Ex. 15).

(*b*) In *Allegro* the fingers must tend to rush on prematurely from the barely achieved note to the next, without any delay, as if intent on lightening the whole passage.

52   Mozart: Figaro Overture

(*c*) CHANGES OF BOWING, POSITION, AND STRING

1. *Changes of bowing.*

Upbow and downbow.

Changes of bowing naturally tend to take place in accordance with the natural tendency of the upbow towards *crescendo* and of the downbow, beginning with an accent, towards *decrescendo*. Both tendencies correspond to the natural course of phrases when the upbow coincides with inhalation, and the downbow with exhalation. But when they do not coincide, the utmost care must be taken not to misrepresent the sense of the music by blindly following the usual course.

Phrasing and bowing.

The prevailing custom of associating the beginning of bars with down-bow leads to most inappropriate phrasing. For instance, the following passage is always played downbow–upbow. But the phrasing obviously requires upbow–downbow. To follow the usual procedure mechanically is to go against a fundamental law; for then, the theme will of necessity sound thus:

53   Beethoven: Violin Concerto, 1st Movement

instead of its immanent tension-*crescendo* being clearly brought out, thus:

54

Upbow and phrase-upbeat.

Conversely, the stereotyped association of upbeat and upbow may result in perfectly ludicrous accentuations and *crescendos*. The beginning of the slow movement in Beethoven's C minor Symphony is always heard approximately thus: the E flat lightly accented, the whole upbeat emphasized. But the tendency of the phrase is a concealed tension-*crescendo*, which proceeds over the A flat to the C, leading to the F in the next bar:

55   Beethoven: 2nd Movement of Vth Symphony

Imagination and technique of bowing.

Variations of length of bowing and pressure.

The cause of these common evils is the lack of a technique of bowing determined by the data of musical imagination and nothing else. This technique requires that the utmost variety of lengths of bowing should be used. The length should increase in proportion as phrasing and *crescendo* move forwards, and decrease as a phrase nears its end, or a *decrescendo* occurs. If in order to ensure quality of tone, one insists on the players using long strokes as much as possible, then, increase of the length of the stroke will mean additional pressure (as expressed in the rising gradation: gliding, drawing, stroking); and, correspondingly, the *decrescendo* will mean a decrease of pressure (as expressed in the falling gradation: stroking, drawing, gliding).

Possibilities of the bow stroke.

Every player must spontaneously realize how vital it is to use the bow appropriately, and consciously to use, as the case may be, full-length, half-length, third-of-the-length strokes, the point, middle, or nut of the bow, upbowing or downbowing, gliding, drawing, or stroking. But consider the actual facts: it very seldom occurs that a player in an orchestra, when giving out a long, increasingly sustained singing cantilena, really knows how to apply to the building-up of it all the possible phases of bowing.

Without exception, changes of bow should never give rise to unrequired accentuations or caesuras. The ideal to be achieved is that of perfect singing, and all technical processes must become subservient.

2. *Change of position.*

The part played by changes of position in melody-building does not call for so much attention as we have devoted to bowing. Every player is aware that changes of position often result in disturbance of the flow, wrong breaks, or wrong accents; all these faults may be avoided either by dint of technical skill or by resorting to a different fingering.

Phrasing and fingering.

(1) A particularly dangerous passage is the descending melody of the first violins in 'Siegfried':

56   Wagner: IIIrd Act of 'Siegfried'

Legato and change of position.

(2) A case in point occurs in the Finale of Mahler's Ninth Symphony:

57   Mahler: 4th Movement of IXth Symphony

Evenness and fingering.

(3) Equally important is a well-thought-out fingering in the *pp legato* passage in semiquavers in the first movement of the Ninth Symphony (see Ex. 40). The absolute smoothness and inner restfulness of this passage can only be achieved if the fingering and bowing of all the bow instruments are strictly uniform.

Timbre and change of position.

(4) Beethoven:

58   Beethoven: Great Fugue, Op. 133

45

The leap of a tenth in the violas must be carried out on the D-string to avoid a sudden break in the melody and a considerable change in timbre.

Timbre

Unity of timbre is one of the very important questions that affect bow instruments. Timbre essentially depends upon which strings are used in the course of a melody. Take, for instance, the above-mentioned second theme in the *Adagio* of Beethoven's Ninth Symphony. It is given out by the violas and second violins, all playing on the D-string. The positive reason for this choice of string is to achieve a warm, yearning, singing tone in the violins; but it is all-important that the violas should not pass from the mellow D-string to the clearer, nasal A-string. The second violins could play the theme on both strings without its fundamental character being much altered: but if in giving out the uppermost notes the violas pass on to the A-string, these notes will be brought out intensively, and the colour will change; they will assume an importunate tone, incompatible with the character of this dreamy, yearning singing.

Weak and strong positions.

This leads us to consider another important question: the use or avoidance of naturally stronger or weaker notes and positions. In all bow instruments, the most powerful strings are the topmost and lowest. The weakest positions are those implying the use of the middle strings. Melodies which it would be natural to play on the middle strings must often be played on the G-string and, when rising, quickly brought over the A-string on to the E-string, so as to produce a tone strong enough to be heard amidst that of the other instruments.

59   Bruckner: 4th Movement of IInd Symphony

60 Beethoven: Great Fugue, Op. 133

Decreasing the tone.

Conversely, weak positions may be selected for the purpose of either ensuring a suitable volume of tone, or giving a melody its truest character:

61 Kaminski: Magnificat, 2nd part

These chorale-like entries of the first violins (doubled in the upper octave by the flute), almost with the character of a *cantus firmus* beginning on a softly veiled organ-stop, are beautiful when played on the D-string:

62 Schubert: 2nd Movement of B minor Symphony

The need for readjustment.

We are in a bad case when an important passage has to be played in so unfavourable and weak a position that it is impossible to impart the required strength to it.

63 Beethoven: Great Fugue, Op. 133

Here there is no remedy except careful readjusting—keeping down all the other parts—and accentuated rhythmic and general energy in performance.

47

Open strings.

Let it be remembered that the open strings must be avoided in the course of a melody; and, elsewhere, used with caution. For their timbre is clearer and may actually occasion (for sensitive ears) a break in the singing:

64   Reger: Sinfonietta

Here the composer expressly stipulates the use of the fourth finger.

This does not apply when open strings are used for accentuation or underlining, or are used simultaneously with the adjacent stopped string *unisons.*

65   Bruckner: Scherzo of IXth Symphony

3. *Change of string.*

Avoiding all mechanical procedures.

When speaking of *legato* bowing, I called attention to the wrong caesuras and accents resulting from mechanical changes of bowing. A classical case in point is the passage in semiquavers in the first movement of Beethoven's Ninth Symphony to which I have referred several times already. Whenever it is performed, slight *crescendi* and accents crop up as players pass from one string to another. It is only by dint of careful study that this passage can be performed as it should be.

Florid melodic patterns.

The same difficulty arises with florid melodic patterns such as the following in Beethoven's C minor Symphony:

66   Beethoven: 2nd Movement of Vth Symphony

Accompaniment patterns.

(2) Accompaniment patterns in classical music—for instance, the following in the Finale of the 'Jupiter' Symphony:

67   Mozart: Finale of Jupiter Symphony

call for particular lightness of technique. A well-trained, light, and supple hand is required in their performance.

Pizzicato.

(3) Far more difficult is the *pizzicato* as it occurs in the *Adagio* of Bruckner's Second Symphony:

68   Bruckner: 2nd Movement of IInd Symphony

These harp-like accompanying notes, falling as separate drops, are almost impossible to execute as evenly and beautifully as they can be imagined.

(*d*) THE NON-LEGATO STROKE

Two kinds must be distinguished:

1. *The sharply shortened tone*

of which the following variants exist: *Détaché, Martellato, Staccato, Spiccato*; in *Staccato* and *Spiccato* (in this latter, by 'throwing' the bow) several notes may be taken with one stroke of the bow.

Détaché.

69   Méhul: 3rd Movement of IInd
Symphony

Détaché

70   Weber: Oberon Overture

49

Détaché.

71 Beethoven: 1st Movement of
IInd Symphony

Martellato.

72 Strauss: 'Till Eulenspiegel'

Martellato.

73 Bruckner: 2nd Move-
ment of IXth Symphony

Staccato.

74 Weber: Euryanthe Overture

Staccato.

75 Mahler: 1st Movement of IIIrd
Symphony

Staccato.

76 Beethoven: 4th Movement of
1st Symphony

Spiccato (natural).

77 Beethoven: Scherzo of IXth Symphony

Spiccato (natural).

78 Rossini: Overture, 'La Gazza Ladra'

Spiccato (natural).

79 Wagner: Meistersinger Overture

Spiccato (thrown, in one bow).

80 Rossini: Wilhelm Tell Overture

Spiccato (thrown, in one bow).

81 Cherubini: Overture, 'Ali Baba'

50

2. *The soft stroke*

may take the form of separate, unaccented strokes (when several notes are included in one such stroke, we have the *Portato*), or of strokes following one another without a break:

Separated.   *Separated.*

82 Haydn: Andante of   83 Weber: Euryanthe Overture
'Paukenschlag' Symphony

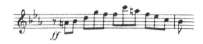

Portato.

84 Beethoven: 1st Movement of Ist Symphony

3. *The soft stroke in unbroken continuity* (see Ex. 42).

The conductor must see to it that these differentiations in bowing are actually utilized. There exists such a wealth of possibilities in the performance of melodies, that the subtlest shadings of tone are needful; but these are often missed by a lack of technical proficiency.

Accuracy of indications in scores.

To realize how carefully composers consider the possibilities of bowing and use them in melody-building, look at the score of the **Oberon Overture**. The beginning of the *Allegro* is an object-lesson in the cumulative use of *staccato*, *legato*, and separate strokes in a *crescendo*, so as to achieve strong definition and a fervid impetus carrying the pattern to its climax:

85 Weber: Oberon Overture

(*e*) THE PIZZICATO

The *pizzicato* (i.e. the production of tone not with the bow, but by plucking the strings with the finger) usually occurs in orchestral playing

51

only under its ugliest form: as a dry snap, a mere noise, breaking into the music. But the *pizzicato* is of noble descent, and its worthy function is to replace the lutes and harps, i.e. instruments whose notes keep their vibrations going for a length of time.

There are various ways of executing it.

Drawing out.

(1) By pressing the fingers against the strings and then softly raising them:

86   Beethoven: Violin Concerto, 1st Movement

Plucking the strings.

(2) By gently plucking the strings with the soft, fleshy part of the finger-tips:

87   Beethoven: Adagio of IXth Symphony

(3) By sharply tugging at the strings with the finger-tips:

89   Reger: Sinfonietta, 4th Movement

88   Wagner: Tristan Prelude

90   Casella: Italia

52

Combinations.

Making motifs stand out.

By combining processes 1 and 2 in *p dolce*, it is possible to bring out a motif in a part, or to carry the tone down to vanishing-point. The accompaniment *pizzicato* in example 91 is to be played *pp* throughout, process 1 being use. Usually, one hears, at bars 7 and 8, the first and second violins standing out quite senselessly, while the 'celli and basses are carrying the theme to its close. Let the lower instruments apply process 2 to these two bars, while the violas and violins stick to process 1. Then the last notes of the theme will remain perceptible, the upper instruments no longer standing out.

91   Beethoven: Allegretto of VIIth Symphony (bars 7–8)

Decrescendo.

To carry out the *decrescendo* in the next example, let process 2 be applied at first to the *pizzicato* notes, and gradually verge towards process 1, so that at the end of the *perdendosi*, the notes are drawn from the strings in the faintest of whispers.

92   Beethoven: Violin Concerto, 2nd Movement

'*Pedal*' *effects.*

The *pizzicato* requires a prolonged vibration of the strings, to which effect the left hand must actively co-operate in the production of the tone. Its fingers must hold the strings down firmly so as to allow full

53

freedom of action to the vibrating part, exactly as an open string vibrates and resounds unimpeded up to the nut of the finger-board. This pedal-like tone is, in the immense majority of cases, the ideal *pizzicato* tone. It is brought out by a *vibrato* of the left hand.

(*f*) THE VIBRATO

Intensity of tone.

The *vibrato* helps to raise the intensity of expression and the colour of the tone, and causes the strings to vibrate to the very end. It should be noticed that it may be more, or less, energetic. An energetic *vibrato* should accompany the silky *p* stroke ('glissez avec l'archet de toute sa longueur') in Stravinsky's 'Histoire du Soldat' so as to give its full value to the soft, repressed, murmured 'Dies Irae':

93   Stravinsky: 'L'histoire du soldat'. Tango

Sensuous intensification of tone.

The climax of the great singing melody in Strauss's 'Don Juan' calls not only for an ever-increasing fullness of tone, but for an increasing *vibrato*, so that at each apex all the sensuously stirring qualities that tone possesses are employed to their utmost:

94   Strauss: 'Don Juan'

Expressive intensification.

The following progression must be performed similarly; but the melodic ascents demand soulful, flowing, singing tone instead of the sensuous outburst in 'Don Juan':

54

95 Reger: Sinfonietta, 3rd Movement

Tone-colour.

The *vibrato*, colouring the tone in the high-pitched passages for 'cello of Beethoven's 'Grosse Fuge', serves to impart to the theme, sung *pianissimo*, characteristic penetrating sweetness which contrasts with the character of the other parts:

96 Beethoven: Great Fugue, Op. 133

Tone-characterization.

The *mf* melody in Glinka's 'Ruslan and Liudmila', performed with the support of quick *vibrati*, acquires a delightful gliding lightness and swing:

97 Glinka: Overture, 'Ruslan and Liudmila'

Effects of registration.

In the Finale of Bruckner's Second Symphony the floating *pp* chords acquire, by the use of a suitable *vibrato*, the character of a softly throbbing echo-stop on the organ, contrasting with the calm, static harmonies in the wind instruments, the equivalent of an entirely different stop:

98 Bruckner: 4th Movement of IInd Symphony

Non-Vibrato.

The opposite effect consists in absolutely excluding the *vibrato*. Thus the stillness of the four-bar transition in Busoni's 'Turandot' (see Ex. 39) becomes even more pronounced and oppressive. Similarly, the dark *morendo* of the E flat minor in Schönberg's 'Verklärte Nacht' can be given the absolute colour of night and immobility by excluding all *vibrato* and playing all the notes of the chords on the lowest strings:

99   Schönberg: 'Verklärte Nacht'

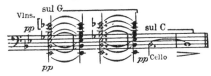

(*g*) COL LEGNO; SUL TASTO; SUL PONTICELLO; TREMOLO

1. Col legno.

Col legno bowing may be a stroke or an impact. The impact with the point may be used as a step above the *pp pizzicato*, to emphasize the march-character of a passage, and simultaneously volatilize the sonority:

Dematerializing the Sonority.

100   Busoni: 'March' (No. 4) from 'Turandot'

Tone-painting.

Mahler uses the impact *col legno* for characterization, and tone-painting, in the 'Sermon to the Fish' in his Second Symphony:

101   Mahler: 3rd Movement of IInd Symphony

and in the Scherzo 'What the Flowers tell me' in his Third Symphony:

102   Mahler: 2nd Movement of IIIrd Symphony

sempre col legno

The *col legno* stroke imparts a glassy character to the sonority.

2. *Sul tasto, sul ponticello.*

Tone-painting. Colouring a melody.

The *sul tasto* plays a far more important part in music than the *sul ponticello*. The latter is hardly used except for *tremoli*; it adds strength to the tone, rendering it shrill and glassy in the *f*, glittering in the *p*. In other words it stands for tone-painting effects. But the *sul tasto*, which diminishes the strength of the tone, is used for colouring melodies. To the natural *decrescendo* scale from bridge to finger-board corresponds a range of colours extending from a glassy shrillness and glitter in *f* to a subdued veiled gloaming in *p*. A good artist will instinctively avail himself of both possibilities when developing intensification, or decreasing the volume of the resonance and intensity of the tone. For instance, in the above-quoted passage from Schönberg's 'Verklärte Nacht', he will play *sul tasto* besides playing *pp*, *non vibrato*, and on the lowest strings.

When the composer does not prescribe special processes, the conductor, guided by his musical imagination, has to determine whether they may prove useful and apply them independently, as natural aids to tone-differentiation. A distinction should be made, of course, between the 'exposed' extreme values of *sul tasto* and *sul ponticello*, which are seldom resorted to, and the approximations to these which have to be used almost constantly in performance.

3. *Tremolo.*

A *tremolo* can be played with the point, the middle, or the nut of the bow, *legato* or *non legato*; and the notes can be either in strictly determinate number or in indeterminate multitude. Let it be noted that not only can differentiations be made in the degree of density or speed, but the utmost variety of character can be achieved by the use of all kinds of *non-legato* strokes.

FINAL REMARKS

TECHNIQUE AND ITS APPLICATIONS

Shades of loudness (*ff*, *f*, *mf*, *p*, *pp*) must be kept distinct from one another. Care should be taken that a sustained *f* in slow downbowing should not turn into a *decrescendo* as the point is reached; and, conversely, that a sustained *p* or *pp* in upbowing should not become louder as the nut is reached.

The players must be capable of maintaining the same degree of loudness during the same time while using different lengths of bowing— sometimes slow-moving pressure near the nut, sometimes quicker stroking with half the length of the bow, or with the quickly drawn whole length of the bow.

Let all possibilities of shading be taken into account: they may be resorted to in all kinds of combinations, in the performance of almost any work, provided only that the players are not hampered by technical shortcomings or habits.

Pauses.

The *crescendo* may be increased by gradually bringing the bow towards the bridge; and conversely, the *decrescendo* may be accentuated by bringing it towards the finger-board. These resources are valuable when the tone has to die out during a pause, or to be increased in sustained final notes.

Strengthening the tone by changes of bowing.

Frequent, various changes of bowing serve to increase the *ff* on one note; by playing several notes in one stroke, the softest *pp* can be achieved. A common mistake to avoid is that of using many changes of bowing in the performance of all sustained *ff* final chords. An even, energetic, slowly drawn *ff* without change of stroke gives the tone an altogether particular and almost unvarying consistency and impenetrability.

PREPAREDNESS IN MUSIC

Being ready to play.

It is important that the players should be ready, both outwardly and inwardly, at the moment of beginning to play and in view of all the problems that crop up in performance. In music (which is the only art whose presentation takes place in time) not enough importance is given to this 'beforehand' attitude in the matter of the players' imagination and self-observation. Luminous, spirited performances are invariably ascribed to instinctive genius. Instinct is one element of the organic, basic secret, of personality; and it cannot be 'learnt'. But it remains helplessly restricted in its manifestations if its possessor is unable to master the needful technique. And in order to master it, he must be aware of all artistic events and actualities past or new.

Significance of the Beginning.

The beginning of a piece may be *p*, or *pp*, or *f*, or *mf*; it may be gentle, agitated, buoyant, or hard; dark and restrained in colour, or bright and exuberant; its character may be that of an insignificant accompaniment; it may give out the constructive energy of the piece in motto-like unison; it may, in short, be as diverse as life itself, and reflect any of life's variations.

How to achieve this.

The conductor must, in one act of tense concentration, immediately seize the personalities of the orchestra and get them under his sole control. When he is ready to raise his stick, every player must have his instrument, ready to play, in front of him. And the conductor's first movement must be so precise, so charged with the required volitional power, as to take effect with the inevitability of a switch turning on electric light.

Technical aids.

Should the music begin with an imperceptible *piano*, the players should be made to start moving their bows (though hardly noticeably) before they actually have to touch the string; the bow, gliding through the air, will gently start impelling the string to vibration. If the beginning is in a natural, simple, singing tone, let the usual practice of accentuating the attack be avoided. If the beginning is energetic, and has to gather up all the forces from the outset, let adequate preparations bring out these forces with the very first note. All these externals should exhibit the accuracy of perfect machinery set in action by the guiding will-power of the conductor.

LEADER AND ORCHESTRA

Educational activities.

It is the duty of the leader, by his influence and watchfulness, to do away with all the usual habits of the string-players and the usual effects of their bad technique. The following are important points:

Downbowing must not emphasize, nor accentuate, nor end in *decrescendo*.

Upbowing must produce no *crescendo*; in upbeats the whole length of the bow need not always be used.

Changes of bowing should never occasion caesuras or accents.

The bow must be used in all suitable ways, all lengths and parts of it being resorted to (nut, point, middle, upper half, lower half).

The various types of *non legato* should be accurately differentiated: *spiccato* should never become *portato*, nor *portato* become *legato*.

As a general law, the stroke in orchestral playing should be the whole-length stroke, in *p* as in *f*, in *dolce* as in *appassionato*; it should resolve all melodies into elastic subdivisions, according to the structure of each one.

The tone must always be intense, never dull—to this effect, the part played by the left hand is vital.

Any technical process must be applied simultaneously by all players: few are the cases when a variety of processes is admissible.

Regulating the divisi, *&c.*

The leader (in association with the principals of the second violins, violas, 'celli, and double-basses) has to regulate the allocation of *divisi* and the distribution of chords and double stops which are impossible to perform undivided. He must come to an agreement with his colleagues on matters of fingering and bowing so far as these are not prescribed by the conductor.

Chamber-music, solo, and orchestral playing.

He must devote special care to the differences between pure orchestral playing and chamber-music or solo playing. All three types occur in the performance of orchestral works; in certain works, all three must be resorted to; in others, perhaps, only one. But every player in the orchestra must be quite at home in all three, so that, for instance, the direction 'Chamber-music playing!' for the performance of a Haydn Symphony will forthwith determine a certain style; that 'solo' playing of brilliant exposed patterns will give the required brightness to passages that would otherwise sound dull; and that the direction 'orchestral playing' should establish the symphonic character of the work performed.

The orchestra's artistic conscience.

Whereas the conductor embodies the spiritual force that gives form to the work, the leader embodies the orchestra's artistic conscience. With the help of the principals, he prepares a flawless instrument. All the players should learn from him that the one object of all technique is to serve, and that its thoughtless or clumsy application robs the sensitive delicate organism of music of its soul. Only thus will it become possible to call forth all the powers, the spiritual energies of music—unimpeded by technical conditions—that are waiting to be awakened. Only then will the orchestra disclose all its riches, only then will the community that is the orchestra, as willed by the conductor, embody the most individual and exalted vitality of every one of its members.

II. THE WIND INSTRUMENTS

A. *THE WOODWIND*

1. TONE PRODUCTION AND BREATHING

A NUMBER of faults which regularly recur in the playing of the woodwind are due to wrong use of the breath. Exactly as with the bow-instruments the bow is often used without the needful differentiations—e.g. an upbeat of one crotchet is given the same length of the bow as a following dotted minim—so do woodwind players use their breath far too uniformly. A short *p* phrase does not require the same volume of air as a long, *legato, f* melody; a shrilly rushing run does not call for the same use of the breath as a quietly undulating, song-like passage; and the same remark applies to the salient notes of exposed registers and the normal or dull positions respectively. The expert virtuoso will always fill his lungs with the same volume of air, but will sensitively vary its use. The volume of air concentrated determines the possibilities of tension, and represents the power-reservoir of tone; the volume blown out corresponds to the bow of the string instruments, with its fine shades of stroking, drawing, gliding, full-length, half-length, &c.

As a rule wind instruments—as compared with bow instruments—mark too few caesuras. For instance, often the accompanying rhythm in the second movement of Beethoven's violin concerto is so blurred that the semiquaver is hardly heard:

103   Beethoven: 2nd Movement of Violin Concerto

Again, often two separate notes of the same pitch are not properly detached from one another and sound as one continued note:

104   Bruckner: 1st Movement of VIIIth Symphony

What happens in both cases is that the players fail to attack the note distinctly.

(1) *Attacking.*

There are two kinds of attack: one that takes place unnoticeably, the other is definite and sharp.

1. The unnoticeable, practically exhaled attack is used:

(*a*) for perfectly *legato* entries without accentuation or any sharpness of attack, as in the following passage of Beethoven's Choral Symphony, in which the flute comes in against the melody of the horn as a reflecting coloration:

105   Beethoven: 3rd Movement of IXth Symphony

(*b*) for instrumental patterns merging into one another and intended to form an uninterrupted chain of sound:

106   Stravinsky: Andante of IInd Suite for small Orchestra

(*c*) in order to introduce rest-like interruptions within the course of a soft *portato*:

107   Haydn: 2nd Movement of E flat major Symphony ('Paukenwirbel')

But here, the process comes very near to that of sharply defined attack: indeed, as often as not, both processes are mingled. The flutist articulates *hty, hty, hty,* while the oboist from time to time uses *h* after *tü.*

(2) *Sharp Definite Attack* (*Tonguing and Articulation*).

This is achieved by means of *tü, dü,* or *doo*; *tü* is used for producing a harder, precise tone, *doo* for a contrasting, softer tone.

Definite attack produces accents, and all kinds of *non-legato* tone: *marcato, staccato,* detached notes, &c. Repeated definite attacks are achieved without the flow of the breath being interrupted.

63

108   Beethoven: Scherzo of IXth Symphony

on signs) and)(
see p. 102 *infra*.

But when it is interrupted, the repeated attacks gain a new significance with regard to phrasing. In the following example, at 1 and 3 there must be a new attack but no interruption of breath; whereas at 2 and 4 the player must breathe as well as re-attack; for there is no break of the *legato* at 1 and 3—merely an articulation of periods, whereas at 2 and 4 the secondary curves of the melody are separated from one another:

109   Beethoven: Violin Concerto, 3rd Movement

Attacks associated with breathing must be timed accurately enough never to take place at the expense of the note attacked. This is one of the chief faults committed by wind players; it results in a drag, in an untidy entry, and a lack of accuracy in what follows. The ideal would be for a player to breathe while accurately phrasing, as an ideal singer does, and never at the expense either of the preceding or of the following note. But to make matters easier, one may allow a minimum of shortening as in the following example:

110   Beethoven: Prometheus, No. 8

A breathed, detaching attack may at times be used even when it seems to go against the phrasing, but really in order to give the phrasing sharper definition:

111   Strauss: 'Don Juan'

Here the breathed attack reinforces the motion up to the B, and gives animation to the transition from the minim to the triplet, which might easily be clumsy.

Again, it may serve to mark subdivisions in the course of a phrase:

112   Schönberg: Chamber Symphony

Here the repetition ⟨notation⟩ reinforcing the statement of the motif, often sounds dull, as a mere tailing-off of ⟨notation⟩, whereas its real function is to gather this first statement up and swing it towards the climax at the beginning of the third bar.

(3) *Special Difficulties of Articulation.*

Care must be taken to see that the players are capable of executing a good *staccato*, double-tonguing and triple-tonguing.

A quick *staccato* is achieved by means of *ti-ti-ti-ti*:

113   Mozart: Jupiter Symphony, Finale

The double push of the tongue, by means of *tiki-tiki-tiki*.[1]

---

[1] The double and triple push of the tongue are taught in the French and Belgian schools of oboe and bassoon as a matter of course. They ensure great advantages, and a particular lightness; so that the study of these methods should be insisted upon despite all objections.

A test of efficiency on this point is the dreaded passage for bassoon in the Finale of Beethoven's Fourth Symphony:

114   Beethoven: IVth Symphony, Finale

An easier way of playing it is: *ta-ta-ti-ke, ta-ta-ti-ke, ta-ta-ti-ke, ti-ke-ta-ta, ti-ke-ta-ta.*

The triple tonguing is either clear coloured, *tikiti—tikiti—tikiti*—as in the fiery, exciting accompanying triplets in the first theme of Strauss's 'Don Juan':

115   Strauss: 'Don Juan'

or darker, *titiki—titiki—titiki.*

In the above example, an easier method of performance is by double-tonguing with accentuation: *tiketi—ketike.*

(4) *The mouthpiece.*

The tone depends upon the mouthpiece itself (in oboes, bassoons, &c., the reed), the position of the lips, and the way of using the mouthpiece. The oboe, clarinet, and bassoon players, by intelligent and careful selection of reeds, will be able to vary their tone, not only for a whole movement, but also during a movement. For instance, at the beginning of the 'Euryanthe' Overture, oboes and clarinets must use their strongest reeds in order to achieve a measure of balance with the tone of the horns and trombones supplying the harmony:

116   Weber: Euryanthe Overture

But at the beginning of Haydn's 'Paukenwirbel' Symphony, the bassoons must use their weakest reeds so as to moderate the natural loudness of their low register.

117 Haydn: Symphony, E flat major ('Paukenwirbel')

In order to change a reed or a mouthpiece quietly in the course of play, oboes and bassoons require three or four seconds, and the clarinet even less—that is, from two to three of the *alla breve* bars at the beginning of the 'Euryanthe' Overture. The change is so speedily achieved, that one can but wonder why the use of a variety of reeds is not more carefully insisted upon, and experimented in.

One must also take care that the players should decrease or increase the length of reed in their mouth according to the required tone-character. Otherwise, it may happen that an excellent oboe player, because he keeps the reed too deep in his mouth, will always give out a thick and loud tone however musically he plays; and another, who mainly uses the tip of the reed, will give out a tone that may be intense and sweet, but will often remain too thin.

In the flute the mouth-hole corresponds to the reed mouthpiece of oboes and bassoons. A natural idiosyncrasy of the instrument is that its low notes tend to be too flat, and its high notes to be too sharp. The player must correct this by nearly covering the mouth-hole with his lips when playing high notes, so as to allow little room for the egress of the air; and when playing low notes, by leaving the mouth-hole free so that the air may rush out in greater volume.

The players' physical idiosyncrasies must be taken into account: an oboist with weak lips requires a bigger reed, and produces a thinner, lighter tone than one whose lips are strong; and therefore all technical resources and varieties and means of reciprocal support must be called into play, so that he will be able to do exactly what is required of him as the conception of the work dictates.

2. VARYING THE TONE

The composer fulfils his intentions by resorting to suitable registers of the instruments; the player fulfils his by imparting colour to the tone he produces. There is no interchangeability of registers (that is to say, there is no possibility of performing a given phrase either in a naturally weak or in a naturally powerful register, as can often be done on bow-instruments). But the tone may be thick or thin, hard, dull, or *dolce* in colour, it may be made to hover or to be squeezed out; it can be extended to emphasize the *legato*, or 'lightening' may be resorted to, rendering it volatile. The first condition of perfect *legato* is that the first note should still be vibrating when the next is forming; and perfect *staccato* calls not only for sharp *tü* attack, but for an immediate holding back of the breath. Between the two extremes there is a whole range of variants; half-way is the *portato* (produced by a fresh attack for each consecutive note, in combination with a continuously maintained *legato* stream of air).

Comparative power of woodwinds.

The particular charm, but also the weakness of the woodwind quartet consists in its dynamic inequality, which is so great that it makes itself felt in any four-part passage for flute, oboe, clarinet, and bassoon. Here is a signal case in point, from the second movement of Hindemith's Piano Concerto:

118   Hindemith: Chamber-music No. 2, 2nd Movement

The G sharp of the flute lies in a naturally dull register, whereas the E of the oboe is naturally sonorous; correspondingly, the F sharp of the bassoon, a high, exposed note, is stronger than the A sharp in the natural medium register of the clarinet. If the four instruments give out the same *p*, the result will be dynamic unevenness of sonority, and, moreover, differently intensive tone-colours of the various instruments, creating further differentiations. In order to achieve an even balance of tone in the performance of the above passage, we must accurately gauge the distinctive natural power of each instrument, the difference in tone-power of its several registers, and the tone-colours which make up each note and create differentiations in intensity; we must insist, accordingly, upon players carefully listening to one another and suitably adjusting their tone.

Hindemith, who knows all instruments and the relationship of their tone to perfection, was, of course, fully aware of the difficulties of this passage in chords for the woodwind. This is clearly proved by the fact that in the *ff* passages, he gave the melody to the oboe (which in this register is more intensive) playing above the flute. But the principle that guided him in writing the passage was to use precisely these four instruments and to achieve a soft, even medium of tone for all four characteristic tone-colours.

Let us now consider a number of differences in the natural degrees of force of the various instruments—differences which are always recurring and have to be taken into account in performance.

1. *The flute.*

In the following *crescendo* in octaves from 'Tristan' the swelling of the flute tone is stronger and more intensive than that of the clarinet, because its more sonorous, exposed high register is used:

119   Wagner: Tristan Prelude

But even within the compass of one octave the prescribed difference (Ex. 120) between the *p* of the clarinet and the following *pp* reply in the flute will hardly be perceptible, unless the *pp* of the flute be taken as the standard of volume, and the *p* of the clarinet entry regulated accordingly:

120   Mussorgsky: 'The Night on the Bare Mountain'

the natural *p* of the clarinet is more easily produced and softer than that of the other woodwinds; therefore, when flute and clarinet are associated,

69

it is usually the natural degree of loudness of the flute that is taken as the basis; when clarinet and bassoon are associated, it is the power of the bassoon tone.

121   Beethoven: Violin Concerto, 2nd Movement

Here, the first bassoon serves as determinant for the whole chord, because the *p* which it may give out without effort is stronger than that of the clarinet.

The same principle applies to the relation between flute and oboe when the flute plays in the upper octave. For instance, in this alternation in the 'Genoveva' Overture:

122   Schumann: Genoveva Overture

the oboe is relatively too weak.

In the second theme of the *Adagio* in Beethoven's Choral Symphony, the flute must barely indicate the *crescendo*, so as not to interfere with the effect of the final climax of the melody given out by the oboe:

123   Beethoven: IXth Symphony, 3rd Movement

In the next example, the inequality between the *p* of flute, oboe, and accompanying strings respectively is astonishing:

124   Beethoven: 1st Movement of IXth Symphony

The flute and oboe will sound stronger than the *p* of the whole

70

accompanying body of strings, unless they both use almost a whispering, anticipatory mode of playing which will approximate their *legato* to the flowing lightness of the strings.

Equally surprising is the power of the flute, as compared with the horn, in the following example:

125   Stravinsky: Variazione II^a in No. 2 (Gavotta) of Pulcinella Suite

Here, the curious dullness of the weaker reply in the horn results from the fact that the gliding quavers are in the high, exposed register of the instrument, which calls for care in slurring. In the next example, the contrast is still greater because the flute plays in a higher octave:

126   Kaminski: Concerto grosso for 2 Orchestras

Conversely, in Miaskowsky's Seventh Symphony the oboe nearly drowns the quiet muffled tone of the piccolo. Again the contrast is between the intensive register of the one instrument and the dull register of the other.

127   Miaskowsky: VIIth Symphony

But the high notes of the flute *f* are so very powerful, that one single flute or piccolo playing in its exposed high register can reinforce to an incredible degree a whole group of strings:

128   Wagner: Meistersinger Overture

(Alone, the second violins would always sound too weak. The piccolo, with intensive blowing, gives the figure its impetuous energy.)

71

Even more obvious is the reinforcing power of the flute in this sweeping tranquil melody:

129 Reger: Symphonic Prologue

2. *The oboe.*

The following passage sets a novel problem:

130 Stravinsky: Variazione Iᵃ (No. 6, Gavotta) of Pulcinella Suite

Unless the second oboe plays with the utmost lightness, almost *pp*, the passage will remain incomprehensible: the scale-pattern will almost monopolize the listening ear, and its slow *staccato* will prove stronger than the dance-rhythm in the first oboe. New factors of tone-force have cropped up: patterns and the method of execution begin to co-operate in forming impressions of tone-values.

But even when there is no difference of process, differences may exist simply on account of dissimilar note-values:

131 Stravinsky: IInd Suite for small Orchestra, Andante

Here, if both flutes play with exactly the same strength, the upper part will prove perceptibly weaker. And the same preponderance of sustained notes over those that are shorter and constantly shifting is manifest in the following passage:

132 Stravinsky: Variazione IIᵃ (No. 6, Gavotta) of Pulcinella Suite

72

In the next example, from Kaminski's 'Magnificat', the viola, following in thirds the melody in the oboe, may easily drown the latter, even if played quite softly, because of its intensive high pitch. The players, therefore, must listen and adjust themselves to one another:

133   Kaminski: Magnificat

Not only in simultaneous playing, but also in passages where instruments take over from one another, does this principle hold good—as in the following duet-like alternation of oboe and viola:

134   Kaminski: Magnificat

In this passage:

135   Stravinsky: Variazione Iª (No. 6, Gavotta) of Pulcinella Suite

we see differences in the natural intensity of tone of oboe and bassoon respectively. The melody of the oboe, lying in an easy register, will be drowned forthwith if the bassoonist does not play his prominent high notes with the most delicate adaptation and shading.

3. *The clarinet.*

In a combination such as occurs in the 'Grand Choral' in Stravinsky's 'Histoire du Soldat'—where the melody is given out by the clarinet over the bassoon, the trumpet, and the trombone, which are marked as playing in exactly the same *f*—the utmost care must be given to inter-adjusted shading for the four-part writing to be clearly heard. Here all the factors considered above come into play: exposed or dull registers, high and low

73

notes, naturally weaker or stronger tones, differences in note-values, contrasting directions of motifs. This piece is worth studying carefully and thoroughly from the practical point of view; for an ideal balance of its tone-forces depends upon the solution of many problems of tone-balance.

The *p* of the clarinet being, as already mentioned, light, it is important that it should not be started too feebly—especially before a *decrescendo* that has to prepare a softer entry of the bassoon:

136 Beethoven: 2nd Movement of Pastoral Symphony

The same remark applies to the final bars of the second movement of Brahms's Third Symphony. There, again, the convenient *p* of the bassoon must be taken as the standard, so as to make possible a *decrescendo* of the four-part phrase, evenly progressing to the very end.

4. *The bassoon.*

It is particularly difficult for a bassoonist to play low notes *p* without strain. It is very seldom that in the opening of the Faust Symphony, the following phrase:

137 Liszt: Faust Symphony, 1st Movement

can be played exactly as prescribed by the composer. Instead of the *perdendo* while the melody sinks to the deep E, one generally hears a pressing on, a perceptible increase in tone. The difficulty of getting the tone to die out after the beginning *piano* (in a register which in itself is weak) can only be overcome by adjustment: let the clarinet, immediately after the accent on the D flat, start a *decrescendo* at once, so that meanwhile the bassoon may enter at least *mp* instead of *p*.

Conversely the bassoon, in its high register, must remain thin in tone if its nobility is to be preserved and comic or coarse effects are to be avoided. For this reason, in the following passage, the *crescendo* cannot, without strain, be carried beyond a restricted *f*: accordingly, the introductory *crescendo* of the flute and second violins must be carefully adjusted and kept within bounds:

138   Strauss: 'Till Eulenspiegel'

In Stravinsky's 'Pulcinella' Suite, the horn and bassoon have to give out the theme as follows:

139   Stravinsky: Pulcinella Overture

Between the upper G of the bass clef and the D above, the bassoon is weak: therefore the notes with which it takes up the melody from the horn must be played a full degree more heavily than is prescribed, so as to carry the motif to its conclusion without decreasing its values.

3. AIDS TO VARIATION OF TONE

Reinforcing the natural tone-strength.

The easiest way of counteracting weaknesses of tone, as already mentioned, is to use a greater degree of force corresponding to what the ideal conception suggests. But in the following paragraphs systematic methods of raising to the required degree sonorities which otherwise would prove weak will be considered.

1. *Accent and breathed attack.*

Both these means serve to bring out melodic and rhythmic patterns. In the next example, the call-motif is to be emphasized by an accent and a breath $\left(\right)$, whereby the fact is emphasized that the attack in the woodwind and the upbeat in the strings form a rhythmic whole:

140   Beethoven: Pastoral Symphony, 1st Movement

When strings start a motif on the downbeat and wind instruments join on with upbeats, the combined effect is far more forcible if these upbeats are accented:

141   Beethoven: Pastoral Symphony, 1st Movement

Breathing-pauses before the attack must help to reinforce the accents in passages such as the following, in order to impart the requisite strength of tone:

142   Hindemith: Chamber-music No. 1, 1st Movement

2. '*Whistling*' *and* '*rolling*'.

As regards the flute especially, a useful device is to 'whistle out' important notes in the following passages, in which this instrument takes the lead and might otherwise be too weak:

143   Weber: Euryanthe Overture

76

144   Stravinsky: Pulcinella (No. 3) Scherzino

Likewise for the insistent calls in the Trio of Beethoven's Pastoral Symphony:

145   Beethoven: Pastoral Symphony, 3rd Movement

The following 'turns' in the first movement of the same symphony approach closely to a 'rolling' of the tone:

146   Beethoven: Pastoral Symphony, 1st Movement

So does this flourish in Hindemith's 'Chamber-music No. 1':

147   Hindemith: Chamber-music No. 1, 1st Movement

Another case in point is the quick trill (whose effect on unsophisticated listeners is infallible, and which may be performed *crescendo*):

148   Kaminski: Magnificat

3. *Forcing the tone (staccato, marcato, &c.).*

Let the quaver triplets accompanying the first theme in Strauss's 'Don Juan' (see above, Ex. 115), which generally lack impetus, be played in an

77

accurate *staccato* by means of sharp triple tonguing—and the passage will become instinct with power and verve, carried along by the swing of the theme. Another, easier way is to use double-tonguing thus: *ti-ke-ti-ke-ti-ke*.

In the following *crescendo* bar (flute, oboe, and bassoon) the *staccato* must be emphasized by a *marcato* on each note, so as not only to arrive at the more important *staccato* of the strings (*f*, *sf*), but to usher it in properly:

149   Beethoven: Allegretto of VIIth Symphony

In order to bring out the canonic entries at the end of the second movement in Hindemith's 'Chamber-music No 1', the flute and clarinet— which, moreover, are numerically weaker than the string quartet—must reinforce by *marcato* every one of their answering quavers:

150   Hindemith: Chamber-music No. 1, 2nd Movement

Sharp, *marcato*-like forcing will impart the requisite sharpness to the following passage for bassoon:

151   Kaminski: Magnificat

4. *Over-extension.*

The term over-extension means using to the full each metric note-value by the employment of the most evenly flowing singing executions possible. Each note, as long as it lasts, must be given the whole tone-power. Thus passages which generally sound dull may acquire the requisite character and gradation.

152 Beethoven: Violin Concerto, 1st Movement

153 Hindemith: Chamber-music No. 1, 2nd Movement

154 Brahms: IIIrd Symphony, 1st Movement

5. *Consistency of sustained notes.*

This means that sustained notes must be sustained to the full from beginning to end, by an even pressure of air (comparable to the constant pressure of the piston upon the driven column of air in an air-pump).

The sustained notes of the piccolo in the storm in the Pastoral Symphony usually sound either thin and too weak, or shrill and piercing. The requisite tone-character, tending towards the climax, will be obtained as soon as the player achieves 'consistency' of tone.

The same holds good with regard to the final cadence of the flute in the first movement of Beethoven's Fourth Symphony, which dominates everything before the interrupted cadence *p* in A major:

155 Beethoven: IVth Symphony, 1st Movement

79

6. *Intensity in execution.*

The following passages are exemplary cases in point:

(*a*) from Kaminski's 'Concerto Grosso'; the leading flute, with its impassioned song, rises, detached from the even, tender *pp* intermingling of the accompanying parts:

156 Kaminski: Concerto Grosso, 2nd Part

(*b*) from Schönberg's Chamber Symphony: only when the tone of the oboe (and of the 'cello) spreads and glows with ever-increasing eagerness will the singing theme rise luminously, with gentle authority, above the almost bewilderingly complex polyphony:

157 Schönberg: Chamber Symphony

7. *Putting in an unnoticeable onward (or tension) crescendo.*

This is a most useful device and is constantly used, either consciously or unconsciously; we know it already as tension-*crescendo*. It must take place unnoticeably, and only indirectly suggest the impression of a *crescendo* caused by the compulsion of the music.

158 Kaminski: Concerto Grosso

159 Honegger: 'Pacific 231'

160   Brahms: IIIrd Symphony, 1st Movement

161   Mozart: Jupiter Symphony, 2nd Movement

8. *Use of stronger reeds.*

This mechanical resource, already mentioned, should be used with far greater care than is generally the case. Let oboe, clarinet, and bassoon players be reminded, with tireless persistence, to avail themselves of it where it proves suitable.

9. *Raising the bell.*

The same rule applies: let the player grow accustomed to use *every* device that may be of service for the presentment of works, and not despise even this primitive, but most effective, mechanical resource.

Reducing the natural force of the tone.

1. *Whispered tone, breathing the tone without obvious respiration.*

In the following passage from Bruckner's Ninth Symphony, in which the flute sings above the vibrating strings, the whisper-like attack and tone production already referred to must be used, so that the flute part will float ethereally through the pattern:

162   Bruckner: IXth Symphony, 3rd Movement

In the Scherzo of the same symphony, the clarinets accompanying the

81

graceful interchange between oboe and bassoon must enter almost imperceptibly and die out in the same way.

163   Bruckner: IXth Symphony, Scherzo

The same applies to the following entry of the second oboe, which must articulate its four-bar phrase without breathing, and yet in accordance with the slurs:

164   Bruckner: IXth Symphony, Scherzo

In the course of the following flute and oboe passages in the first movement, again there should be no breathing:

165   Bruckner: IXth Symphony, 1st Movement

And in the *adagio*, despite the rests, the flute and clarinet should attack afresh but without breathing, so that the prescribed *decrescendo* will take place more or less of its own accord:

166   Bruckner: IXth Symphony, Adagio

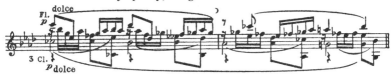

2. *Keeping back the tone.*

By quietly concentrating the breath and reducing the volume of tone-producing air blown, the requisite *sotto voce* of the bassoons at the beginning of the Finale of Brahms's Third Symphony will be achieved:

167   Brahms: IIIrd Symphony, 4th Movement

Likewise with the tender *pp* thirds of the flutes, clarinet, and bassoon in unison, shortly before the end of the same movement:

168   Brahms: IIIrd Symphony, 4th Movement

3. *Slurs.*

There is no need to give any special explanation on this point. Let it be noticed how slurs are used, and what their intended effect is, in the following examples:

169   Stravinsky: 1st Suite, March

170   Bruckner: IXth Symphony, Scherzo

4. '*Lightening.*'

This may occur both in *legato* and detached playing. Contrary to over-extension, 'lightening' aims at filling in the metric note-values as lightly as possible, so as barely to touch on them and pass on to, and over, the next note with similar lightness:

171 Busoni: 'Turandot', No. 1

172 Strauss: 'Till Eulenspiegel'

We also encounter it in the form of nimbly flowing melody:

173 Busoni: 'Turandot', No. 1

or of associated *legato* and *staccato*:

174 Busoni: 'Turandot', No. 2

or in rising and falling blocks of chords:

175 Busoni: 'Turandot', No. 4

or as an extreme form of the lightest *staccato*:

176 Busoni: 'Turandot', No. 8

'Lightening', in association with *staccato*, imparts the requisite sparkling buoyancy to the rhythm of the woodwind in the scene of the Maskers in Strauss's 'Don Juan'.

177 Strauss: 'Don Juan'

5. *Colorations, echo-tone, flageolet-tone.*

The possibility of variously colouring their tone enables the woodwind to make up, in a measure, for the absence of interchangeable dull or sonorous tone for notes of the same pitch. The first conditions for tone-coloration are a discriminating ear and a subtle power of imagining tones. Given these, a good oboist, dealing with the following passage from Kaminski's 'Magnificat' (the bass being in the viola, the harmony provided by two flutes *pianissimo*), will, in accordance with the combination of sonorities preceding his entry, colour it with a thin, sweet, plaintive tone which the viola (in its main capacity of bass) will really be able to support:

178 Kaminski: Magnificat

85

Similarly, in the second movement of Beethoven's Fourth Symphony, the clarinet can bring its tone (the so-called echo-tone) very near to that of the silvery, calm accompaniment (*pizzicato* of the second violins, eked out by grace notes in the first violins):

179   Beethoven: IVth Symphony, 2nd Movement

and at the end of the first movement in Kaminski's 'Magnificat', it can hush its tone and carry it down to a mere sigh:

180   Kaminski: Magnificat

The flute and oboe produce harmonic notes (by over-blowing or by the use of the octave-key) in order further to reduce the tone in final notes dying out *pp*, or to achieve special tone-effects:

181   Stravinsky: 'Pulcinella', No. 3

6. *The* Non espressivo.

This, the avoidance of all expressively stimulant elements in tone, reduces the properties of tone to plain resonance without swelling or *vibrato*. The tone, then, naturally becomes softer, almost thinner:

182   Beethoven: Allegretto of VIIth Symphony

183   Busoni: 'Turandot', No. 8

p e monotono

7. *Deliberate reduction (enfeeblement).*

In passages such as the following, the upward movement of the *pp* quavers, rising to the high F sharp, may easily produce the illusion of a *crescendo*, which can best be prevented by deliberately letting the tone drop:

184   Bruckner: Adagio of IXth Symphony

pp

This resource is particularly valuable in passages tending to bring out ascending final notes—a tendency which in the following example is accentuated by the fact that the last notes are in shorter values:

185   Beethoven: 'Eroica', 1st Movement

p

8. *Changes of reed.*

See what was said on this point, pp. 66–7 *supra*.

9. *Blowing towards the desk. Mutes.*

A natural way of damping consists in directing the wind on to the surface of the desk. But there also exist actual mechanical contrivances for muting:

(*a*) By closing the bell with a cloth (oboe, clarinet, bassoon); a device prescribed by Stravinsky for the clarinet in 'l'Histoire du Soldat', and indicated by the word *coperto* (covered) or with *aperto* (open) to show where it ends. The trouble is that it is impossible to draw out and replace the cloth frequently and quickly; this is easily overcome by having two instruments in each key (B flat and A), one with the bell closed and the other open, ready to hand.

87

(*b*) By means of a mute (for the bassoon). This consists of a brass cylinder filling two-thirds of the breadth of the instrument's funnel, six to eight centimetres long, covered with felt, and its outer end stopped with gauze. When this is used, the particularly dangerous notes C to G in the lowest octave sound very much like the soft *p* notes of a trombone.

4. MAINTAINING THE NATURAL VOLUME

Faulty weakening of tone.

It will now be shown how to avoid unintentional *crescendi* and *decrescendi*.

1. *Allowing the tone to fall.*

The act of blowing naturally tends to become less energetic towards the end of phrases, when the supply of air is nearing exhaustion; and the tone drops accordingly. This tendency, which falsifies the sense of many passages, should be relentlessly countered. The best way is to use an unobtrusive tension-*crescendo*, such as was described as the conscious urge of a melody towards its climax:

186   Beethoven: IXth Symphony, Scherzo

187   Beethoven: IVth Symphony, 1st Movement

2. *Wrong lightening.*

The thrilling unison triplets in Strauss's 'Don Juan' will never have the requisite energy and swing (adequate to that of the string passages) unless lightening is carefully avoided—even in *ff.*

188 Strauss: 'Don Juan'

Likewise as regards the jagged *staccato* motif in Schönberg's Chamber Symphony:

189 Schönberg: Chamber Symphony

and the rushing scales that lead up to the repeat in the 'Euryanthe' Overture:

190 Weber: Euryanthe Overture

3. Insufficient use of breath-phrasing.

Let us take as an example the theme of the first movement of Erwin Lendvai's Chamber Suite, op. 32, which can hardly be played as phrased in the printed edition. Remembering that it is possible to breathe afresh at the expense of a previous note, we may phrase it, let us say, thus:

191 Lendvai: Chamber Suite, I

4. Unequal note-values.

In the following passage for the flute in the first movement of Bruckner's Eighth Symphony, the semiquavers after the dotted crotchets are often hardly perceptible; and then the rising and falling melody is heard not as a whole but as a fourfold repetition. If each semiquaver is given more

89

weight by barely perceptible pressure—by over-extension—the melody will be rounded off, and *decrescendo* gaps avoided:

192   Bruckner: VIIIth Symphony, 1st Movement

5. *Unevenness resulting from differences of process.*

Something similar occurs when we have *legato* and *staccato* simultaneously, as in the Tarantella in Stravinsky's Second Suite, where the first bassoon, *legato*, sounds weaker than the second pursuing its course in the same *p*, but *staccato*:

193   Stravinsky: 2nd Suite for small Orchestra, Tarantella

Faulty increase of force.

1. *Arbitrary, uncalled-for* crescendi.

The fact that *crescendo*, *espressivo*, and ascending motion generally coincide leads to false increase of force in passages like the following:

194   Beethoven: 4th Movement of IVth Symphony

195   Beethoven: IXth Symphony, Adagio

(See also Ex. 168.)

90

2. *Exposed registers producing* crescendo *effects.*

On this point, it is enough to refer to the high notes of the clarinets in D and E flat, and those of the flute, which are naturally loud; and, conversely, to the low, heavy registers of oboe and bassoon.

3. *Rising motion.*

Here, apart from the tendency to associate *crescendo* with upward motion as a matter of habit, there is the fact that in the upper register tone naturally grows louder. The best remedy is to prescribe a *decrescendo.*

196 Beethoven: Pastorale, 1st Movement

197 Beethoven: VIIth Symphony, 1st Movement

198 Stravinsky: 'Pulcinella' Suite, No. 3

4. *Gradual entry of the whole orchestra, group by group.*

It is easy to yield to the tendency to increase the prescribed degree of force, instead of maintaining it unaltered, in proportion as more instruments enter.

5. *Accentuating final notes.*

The tendency to underline the end of a phrase, and to draw attention to it, leads to wrong accents on final notes:

199 Stravinsky: 2nd Suite for small Orchestra, Espagnola

91

5. PURITY OF PITCH

Woodwind players can regulate the pitch of their instruments either by adjusting the length or by altering the position of their lips. Often, single notes will have to be adjusted to one another in the course of a harmonic progression. For instance, even the most careful tuning of the orchestra is no guarantee that the passage from Kaminski's 'Magnificat' quoted example 178 above will sound quite true to pitch unless the oboe and the flutes make certain of it by very carefully listening to one another. It is desirable to give this passage a final test by quickly playing it through just before the performance of the work begins.

Likewise, at the beginning of the Adagio in Hindemith's Piano Concerto (see Ex. 118), the woodwind players must listen keenly if the chord of the ninth (minus the fifth) is to be given out so as fully to develop its beautiful sonority. This chord must be attacked on the sharp side, so as to be capable of including correctly the false diminished fifth given out by the strings *unisono*.

The free *pp* entry of the first oboe on the B flat in the following example is very sensitive (Beethoven's Choral Symphony, Finale, before the words 'O'er the firmament'). This note must be taken with reference to the fact that the note A, which is the root of the chord, will come in shortly, turning the seventh which this B flat constitutes at first into a ninth:

200 Beethoven: IXth Symphony, Finale

We will now deal with a case of salient registers such as occurs in the fifth bar of Schönberg's Chamber Symphony. The work begins with a statement of a chord in fourths, G-C-F'-B♭'-E♭''-A♭'', which resolves after permutations of tension, dissonance and power, on the chord of F major, on which chord all the woodwind come in *piano* ――◁ ▷――. In order to ensure the full effectiveness of the delightful resolution on F major, it is vitally necessary to play dead true to pitch, and, before beginning, once again to test the pitch most carefully. The faintest deviation in any one of the wind instruments, and this wonderful cadence will lose something of its clarity and satisfying charm.

Owing to the materials of which the instruments are made, purity of pitch is easily endangered when instruments such as the piccolo, the D and E flat clarinets, and the double-bassoon join the usual woodwinds; or when, in chords comprising many parts, single notes in exposed registers have to be given out by one or several instruments.

It ought to be possible, in every orchestra, to entrust to the first oboe or the first flute the responsibility for obtaining unimpeachable tuning of the whole woodwind. Let no pains be spared to get players to submit to such an important discipline, under the guidance of one of their number.

6. TONE-COLORATIONS

The possibility of attuning the whole woodwind quartet to the tone-colour of one of its group has so far been overlooked. All four woodwinds can colour a harmonic passage to blend with the tone-colour of the flute, the oboe, the clarinet, or the bassoon; in other words, the whole quartet may do what we have already seen done by two instruments (clarinet and bassoon, or oboe and viola) in the matter of adjustment to one another.

An ideal and highly artistic instance for the practical study of this possibility is afforded by the third of Schönberg's Five Orchestral Pieces, Op. 15, entitled 'Colour Play'. What the composer wants is a movement accomplished not by the usual rhythm-articulation, but by the flash of constantly changing tone-colours over a quiet harmonic foundation.

201   Schönberg: 5 Orchestral Pieces, No. 3

These 'Five Orchestral Pieces' afford good practice in unobtrusive entries and exits; in maintenance of an unstrained, smooth, constant tone, and also (in spite of the greatest differences in instrumental registers and tone-colours) an even basic force; and finally, in the achievement of a most accurate, meticulously tested intonation.

7. APPORTIONED MELODIC PATTERNS

Melodies that are not given out by one soloist throughout, but pass, in subdivisions, from one instrument to another, cannot be correctly performed unless each player mentally sings the whole of them as they are played, and contributes his share in accordance with the conception of the whole thus formed. The misguided spirit of competition among players, and the failure to achieve co-ordination and subordination to the requirements of the melody as a whole, are constant sources of error in this matter.

202   Beethoven: Adagio of IXth Symphony

203   Reger: Sinfonietta, Adagio

204   Beethoven: 'Prometheus', No. 4

But an all-embracing conception is more difficult when the subdivisions of the melody are embedded, almost hidden, within the harmonic tissue. Here it is a matter of adjustment: bringing out the oboes to correspond to the first violins, and keeping down the high notes of the flutes above.

205   Beethoven: Ist Symphony, 2nd Movement

FINAL RECOMMENDATIONS

Even more than with bow instruments, it is all-important that wind players should possess, and use, first-class instruments. Let no means be neglected of checking the deplorable custom of using inferior instruments for orchestral playing, while keeping good instruments for private use. It is also useful to encourage all players who make their own slips or reeds for pleasure by showing interest in their activities. It would be ideal if each player was able to manufacture the kind of slips and reeds best adapted to his requirements and exactly corresponding to his own idiosyncrasies. All players of the same instrument should at any rate have instruments of identical manufacture. As with the strings, there should be no marked difference in quality between firsts and seconds. One single potential mischief-maker among the woodwind, and the beauty of tone and, first and foremost, the purity of intonation of the whole group will ever be trembling in the balance. Let great care be taken that the players of supplementary instruments (piccolo, cor anglais, clarinets in **D** and **E** flat, double-bassoon) be first-rate artists, playing faultless instruments and given to constant practice of them despite their secondary character; thus, at long last, the terrible anxieties experienced by orchestras and conductors whenever any one of these instruments has to play in an exposed register will become a thing of the past.

A good way of training the woodwind is to promote solo-playing, either with the orchestra accompanying or in front of the orchestra (a practice that the musicians of the Dresden State Opera House have adopted long since). Let opportunities be created if they are not forthcoming otherwise: popular concerts and practice concerts will serve splendidly. Here again, example is the best means of education; if one or two first-class

95

artists playing the flute or oboe set the example, all the others will gradually learn from them and try in turn to achieve a level above the ordinary.

APPENDIX

REPERTORY OF WOODWIND SOLI WITH ACCOMPANYING ORCHESTRA

FLUTE:

J. S. Bach: Triple Concerto in A minor for flute, clavier, violin, and orchestra.

Brandenburg Concerto in D major for flute, violin, clavier, and strings.

Suite in B minor for flute and string orchestra.

Quantz: Concerto for flute with strings and harpsichord.

Mozart: Flute concertos in D major and G major.

Andante for flute and orchestra.

Concerto in C major for flute and harp with orchestra.

Weber: Romance and Siciliana for flute and orchestra.

Wolfgang von Bartels: Concerto for flute and string orchestra.

Busoni: Divertimento for flute with small orchestra.

OBOE:

Handel: Concerti Grossi Nos. 8 and 9.

Concerti for oboe and orchestra (1738).

Haydn: Concerto for oboe and orchestra.

Mozart: Concerti in F major and E flat major.

d'Indy: Variations for oboe and orchestra.

COR ANGLAIS:

Mozart: Concertante for cor anglais and strings.

CLARINET:

Mozart: Concerto in A major.

Spohr: First, second, and fourth Concerti for clarinet and orchestra.

Weber: Two Concerti for clarinet and orchestra.

Debussy: Rhapsody for clarinet and orchestra.

Busoni: Concertino for clarinet and small orchestra.

BASSOON:

Mozart: Concerto in B flat major for bassoon and orchestra.

Weber: Concerto for bassoon and orchestra.

B. *THE BRASS*

The points of playing, of attack, and of technique mentioned in respect of the woodwind hold good, with slight differences, for all wind-instruments—therefore, for the brass. We can apply to the playing of the brass the recently acquired ideas of lightening and over-extension, and practically all the points of view from which we determined the qualities of, and natural differences between, the several woodwind instruments and their several registers. There is therefore no need to go into details again. A few examples and suggestions will suffice. But it is needful to deal carefully with the peculiarities of the brass.

GENERAL REMARKS

Use of the diaphragm, and exercises in breathing.

In order to handle brass instruments without fatigue, a correct attitude and correct breathing are of paramount importance. Correct breathing depends so much upon a correct attitude, that regular exercises in breathing should be instituted for all players: exercises practised without instrument, with the object of ensuring that the diaphragm is used quietly and powerfully. The player, when sitting erect and playing, must have mastered diaphragm-breathing as string players have mastered the correct holding of the bow; then he will always have an ample supply of air and be able to produce his tone without fatigue.

Standard of players.

Again, care should be taken that there should be no great difference in standard between players. The third, fifth, or seventh horn should be able to fill the post of first horn satisfactorily, and the second trombone should be as good as the first and third.

Wagner tubas.

All the horn-players should be made to practise playing the Wagner tubas regularly, lest through unfamiliarity they should always be nervous when using them, and have to play themselves in laboriously. Incompetent strangers should never be brought in to play the tubas. It is always far easier to find four really useful horn-players from outside than four passable tuba-players. As the tubas are generally the property of concert societies, let care be taken that they be first-class instruments, and kept in good order.

Bass tuba and accessory instruments.

Attention should likewise be paid to the quality of the bass and contrabass tuba and of their players. The old system of 'accessory' instruments is inadmissible in a first-class orchestra.

Neither the bass and contrabass tuba, nor the double bassoon or piccolo are 'accessory' instruments in the modern orchestra—this quite apart from the fact that the standard of playing and players should be uniformly good for all instruments.

Faults in attacking.

The mode of attack should never change in the course of a phrase; for such changes, apart from affecting pitch, bring changes of tone-colour. So far as possible, sudden increases in the pressure of the instrument against the lips should be avoided, as endangering the beauty of the tone. Players should always be made to use the same mode of attack. This holds good even for the horns, despite the old dispute whether the horns should attack sharply or softly. When all is said and done, it is a matter of individual disposition, which may be regulated one way or the other. But the mixture of sharp and soft attack should be excluded for the above-mentioned reasons, though many horn-players attempt this, using the former for high notes and the latter for low.

Pedal notes.

The trombone-players must make an exception when giving out pedal notes: these notes are produced by bringing the lower jaw close, and applying the mouthpiece to the lips particularly lightly, so as to render it possible for the lips to vibrate.

Mode of attack.

For the horn and trumpet, the attack is made by faintly pronouncing a *ta*; for the trombone a *dü* or *doo*, for the bass and contrabass tuba a *tü*.

Double-tonguing and its uses.

In the Middle Ages trumpeters made the technique of double-tonguing (called tongue-beat) a trade secret. As with the woodwind, this device is generally important, and players should be emphatically requested to master it—all the more as it can then be applied in an endless variety of forms. It is executed by means of *ti-ke*, as in the repeated double-tonguing *ti-ke-ti-ke* which we already know. For sequences of three notes it is *ti-ke-ti*; for sequences of four notes, *ti-ke-ti-ke* or *ti-ke-ti-ki*, and of five *ti-ke-ti-ke-ton*. For consecutive triplets double-tonguing is used with the accent thus: *ti-ke-ti*-KE-*ti-ke*, &c.

'Pushing' and 'drawing' out the tone.

The actual attack can take place by 'pushing' the tone or by 'drawing' it out. The latter means the use of an almost whispered *ta* followed by a singing expansion of the tone. There are also the several variants of *legato* and *non legato*, as with the woodwind.

Slurring.

For effecting a *legato*, players use *ta-hi* in upward motion, and *ta-ha* in downward. The trombones, however, use *doo-li* and *di-loo*. Ideal *legato* is rendered difficult when natural notes are to be followed by notes produced by valves, because the use of the valve immediately interrupts the *legato* and can be hidden only by careful practice. In rising patterns (even *staccato*), *i* is universally used for the higher notes; and conversely, *a* is used for going down. With regard to slurs, let it be pointed out that upward leaps call for greater lip pressure and stronger blowing; on the contrary, in downward motions, the lips are relaxed and the wind held back.

Purity of pitch. Use of the lips. Change of grip.

The next question is how to achieve purity of intonation. Sharp notes can be corrected by relaxing the lips, flat notes by increasing their pressure. A change of grip may also help to adjust matters. In every position of the trombones, certain high notes prove out of tune; this can be remedied only by a change of position.

Out of tune notes of the horn may be corrected by the right hand, which is in the bell. Players use this device whenever they have to play stopped notes, because stopping always raises the pitch.

Musicians seldom realize what extreme accuracy of ear is required by

99

players of brass instruments; every stopped note, or note *con sordino*, means *a priori* that purity of intonation may be endangered.

Sources of faults.

The player should be careful not to force the tone in *crescendi*; and even in *f* and *ff* the tone should not be 'driven', otherwise the pitch may easily be affected. Another thing to avoid is the trembling of the lips (*tremolo*) which often takes place in slow and long *crescendo–decrescendo* with players who have not quite mastered the art of tone-production.

Relativity of brass forte.

Great attention must be paid to the use of dynamic indications. The *forte* of the brass is always to be understood as relative. For instance, if the woodwind has to dominate the harmony, the brass must subordinate itself to the woodwind *f*:

206   Beethoven: IIIrd Symphony, 'Marcia Funebre'

Conversely, if the brass enters by way of crowning the climax of the whole orchestra's progression, its *forte* power must be made even more brilliant by intensity of tone, by over-extension, and so forth.

207   Reger: Symphonic Prologue

If the brass only has a motif which passes through various instrumental groups, it must adjust itself to the average *forte* or common standard for all.

208   Beethoven: Vth Symphony, 1st Movement

The diverse character of the brass in the orchestra.

It must first be decided whether the function of the brass is to strengthen the woodwind group and incorporate itself within it (as in Reger's Serenade, Op. 95, in which at times the horns provide soft, pedal-like prolongations of notes, and the trumpets gentle touches of light amid the woodwind group), or to provide light rhythmic accents or allusions to motifs (as in Beethoven's Symphonies and in Mozart's 'Jupiter' Symphony); or whether its part in polyphonic music is merely to provide non-essential harmonic filling-in or to develop thematic, structural elements (Reger, 'Symphonic Prologue').

Time-rate of crescendo *and* decrescendo.

Frequently the *crescendo* and *decrescendo* of the brass must be carried out at a different rate from that of strings or woodwind; for instance, when a composer withdraws the brass, as he would an organ-stop, from a *tutti* so as to let its sonority vanish amid the general sonority, then, having suppressed the woodwind-stop in the same way, allows the softer tone-colour of the strings to continue alone to the end—see the two epilogue-like climaxes in Reger's 'Symphonic Prologue'.

The same process can be carried out in a different manner: with the brass at the climax, the transition in the strings, and the dying-out in the woodwind alone (Toch, Piano Concerto, Second Movement).

English, German, and French brass instruments.

Instruments differ in different countries. In Germany the Wagnerian solemn tone of the trombones has become the standard for all the brass, and the horns belong entirely and solely to the great group rising above their compass—the bass tubas, trombones, Wagner tubas, and trumpets; English trumpets and trombones constitute a distinct family of a clearer tone-colour determined by the brilliancy of the trumpets; and in France horns often sound very much like bassoons, the thinness of their tone being almost incredible to ears accustomed to German horns.

That these differences are not accidental, but originate in the peculiarities of each country's conception of tone, is shown by the comparative study of typical scores—say, of the brass in Wagner or Bruckner's works, in works by Lord Berners or Bliss, and in works by Debussy. Hence it would be very desirable for big concert societies to be able to imitate the

101

example set by the Frankfurt Museumgesellschaft, and have in their possession sets of instruments from various countries so that the true character of the brass be preserved when works from these countries are performed.

The alto trombone.

Every orchestra should possess one of these; it is, even nowadays, indispensable for performing Mendelssohn's 'Ruy Blas' Overture; Schumann's E flat major Symphony; 'Rienzi'; 'La Muette de Portici'; and Bach's 'Art of Fugue' in Wolfgang Gräser's arrangement.

Bass and contrabass tuba.

As regards important tuba parts, it is to be recommended that very deep notes should be taken on the contrabass tuba, and high, exposed notes on the bass tuba. With these two instruments (often neglected by composers) the conductor should be able to use his discretion in the matter of using the one or the other or both alternatively when the score merely prescribes a 'tuba'.

Echo (effect of muting).

Echoes can be given out on all brass instruments. But the directions 'stopped' or '*con sordino*' should be faithfully observed. The two devices produce altogether different effects: stopped notes sound smothered, muted notes have a tender, almost glassy character. Both devices call for a careful control by the ear, and players should be requested to practise them regularly.

Breathing and phrasing indications.

Here again the rule holds good, that breath should not be taken at the expense of the note to come, but at most by a slight, unnoticeable shortening of the note just given out. The conductor should take the trouble to mark the parts with breathing and phrasing signs; these are even more needful to ensure clear performance on the part of the unwieldy brass than they are for the woodwind; in fact, they are as vitally important as indications of bowing for the strings. Let the following signs be used:

) for a fresh attack.

)(for a fresh attack associated with an interruption of breathing.

Technical idiosyncrasies of brass instruments.

A good many of the faults usually committed by players were dealt with in the sections devoted to the woodwind. There are a number of hampering characteristics common to all wind instruments. We shall now deal with a few that are peculiar to the brass.

Late attacks.

Bad starts often occasion a delay in attacking; this fault becomes particularly serious when the entry has to accentuate the first beat of a bar.

209   Stravinsky: Tarantella of 2nd Suite for small Orchestra

Here the tuba, which plays a part similar to that of a bass drum (exactly as in the parallel passage coming afterwards, the trumpet practically plays that of a triangle), may be liable to lag; let the instruments therefore be made to enter exactly at the required moment, even if occasionally this means their having to shorten the preceding note. The same applies to the entry of the tuba, which is far more dangerous—rendered increasingly irritating to players as often as not, by the inconvenient slurring which follows it—in Webern's Op. 6:

210   Webern: No. 2 of 6 Orchestral Pieces, Op. 6

When in the giving out of a motif, after there has been a difference of articulation between the melody and the accompanying parts (as between trumpets and horns in the following example), the parts resume simultaneous motion again, inaccuracies are liable to occur. Here, the horns usually tend to drag after their first long-sustained note:

211   Tiessen: Prelude to a Drama of Revolution

103

When the brass only doubles the 'main notes' of an evenly proceeding pattern, the constantly repeated attacks may easily lead to these notes coming in too late:

212   Beethoven: Scherzo of IXth Symphony

Low notes beginning without noticeable attack, and especially when *crescendo-decrescendo*, can only be given out with the required accuracy if the players carefully time themselves to be there at the right moment:

213   Hindemith: Finale of Chamber-music No. 2

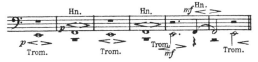

The difficulty of the following slurs leads to hesitation, but by breathing at the right moment (on the end of the foregoing note) the players will be able to take up each fresh slur quietly:

214   Berg: Chamber Concerto for Violin and Piano

In the next example the trumpet has less tendency to drag when entering than when attacking its second D, and the horn less when giving out its first note B than in the difficult slurred pattern that follows:

215   Berg: Chamber Concerto for Violin and Piano

If the players do not accurately understand the two-bar grouping in the following example, the brass will not give out the reply with perfect precision:

104

216   Beethoven: VIIth Symphony, Scherzo

Trpt. and Timp.

Note the tension-crescendo in bars 1 and 3.

The ensemble of the brass, harnessed in the monotonous rhythm of the strings, generally tends to hang back on the single notes, instead of pressing onwards to its third bar (last bar of following example), which makes the climax of the phrase.

217   Stravinsky: 2nd Suite for small Orchestra, Balalaika

Detaching by breathing.

In order to make the canonic repetition of the motif in the low brass distinct, players must not only attack afresh before the crotchet on the fourth beat, but also breathe.

218   Reger: Symphonic Prologue

Detaching by breathing (and the new strength thereby gained) serves to heighten the progression of a motif towards its climax:

219   Reger: Symphonic Prologue

105

The players must also use this method to analyse a melody into its right periods and to carry it towards its goal:

220   Reger: Symphonic Prologue

But one of its chief uses is to bring the rhythmic driving force of a passage to its full *agitato* development:

221   Reger: Symphonic Prologue

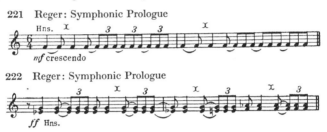

222   Reger: Symphonic Prologue

The next example shows how cleverly Bruckner has succeeded in imparting ever-increasing power to successive rising attacks of a motif, the melodic line proceeding *legato* continuously:

223   Bruckner: IXth Symphony, Adagio

(The effects to be aimed at are: (*a*) forcible attacking of the up-beats—which the horns are able to achieve by breathing because the *legato f* of the trombones and contrabass tuba covers up the gap which this breathing occasions at the end of every bar: (*b*) vigorous emphasis of the main notes—through the accents marked by the trombones and contrabass tuba at the beginning of every bar (after breathing); and (*c*) an unbroken continuity of line in sustained *legato f*.)

Double-tonguing.

A few examples will suffice to show how very important for brass players is a perfect command of the art of double-tonguing. Quadruple beats ($\overset{>}{ti}$-ke-$\overset{.}{ti}$-$\overset{>}{ki}$) occur in Busoni's 'Turandot' Suite—any other way of performing the passage makes it drag and sound clumsy:

224   Busoni: 'Turandot', No. 1

Quintuple beats (ti-ke-ti-ke-ton) occur in Stravinsky's Second Suite, and no other mode of execution will serve as well to give the right expression to the syncopated course of this melody towards its last bar:

225   Stravinsky: 2nd Suite for small Orchestra, Espagnola

Unless the double-tonguing is brilliantly performed, the initial rhythm of the pp trumpet-motif in 'Till Eulenspiegel' and its repetition will never receive their full character of rousing sparkle and perfect ease:

226   Strauss: 'Till Eulenspiegel'

Double-tonguing with the accentuations reversed must be used to impart aggressiveness and driving-power to this sharp 'Tarantella' in triplets:

227   Stravinsky: 2nd Suite for small Orchestra, Napolitana

This virtuoso passage for trumpet in Stravinsky's 'Galop' cannot be performed except by continuous quick double-tonguing:

228   Stravinsky: 1st Small Suite, Galop

107

'Lightening.'

'Lightening' is a more valuable resource for the unwieldy brass than for any other instruments. It can be used in most dissimilar circumstances to achieve the required effect.

The best opportunity for its employment occurs when the music has to go forward relentlessly, unimpeded in its course by any recalcitrant note (here the crotchets and quavers):

229   Reger: Symphonic Prologue

It is even more important to use it when differently moving rhythms and patterns occur together. In a combination of strings and brass like the following, the brass players, by 'lightening', should achieve something of the lightness of the strings, and occasionally an almost *pizzicato*-like tone:

230   Busoni: 'Turandot', No. 2

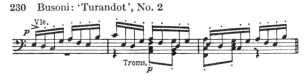

The notorious last bars of Beethoven's Pastoral Symphony call for the utmost lightness and precision of performance on the part of the horns, which should adjust themselves to the quietly gliding strings:

231   Beethoven: Pastoral Symphony, Finale

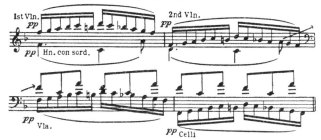

In the Haffner Serenade, horns and trumpets must assume the elegant lightness of the rushing string quavers, so that their main rhythm should not drag by comparison:

232   Mozart: Haffner Serenade, No. 1

When the brass supplies harmonic filling-in for a polyphonic design, all passages whose thickness might lead to a smothering of the other sonorities should be made lighter and more transparent by the same device. As it always causes an urge onwards, it is the best way of preventing lagging motion (such as the usual dropping of short up-beat values). The following are cases in point:

233   Busoni: 'Turandot', No. 1

234   Bruckner: IXth Symphony, 1st Movement

(Note: Ex. 234 illustrates the first sentence, Ex. 233 the second.)

But the greatest value of 'lightening' is that by its use technical unwieldiness and ensuing obstacles to performance can be avoided. 'Rough' slurs (e.g. in octave-leaps of trumpets) can be conceived in quicker values (in the next example, almost as in demisemiquavers) in order to achieve the actual prescribed value easily:

235   Hindemith: Chamber-music No. 1, 1st Movement

109

Big leaps must generally be started and completed in advance of time, so as not to straggle behind the strings proceeding strictly in tempo.

236   Bruckner: IXth Symphony, Adagio

Unusual *legato* slurs (which are seldom encountered) must be carried hastily and lightly to their goal by means of 'lightening':

237   Stravinsky: 1st Suite for small Orchestra, Valse

In the following strict quick march on the trumpet *staccato*-like 'lightening' will impart the requisite buoyancy to the semiquaver triplets and final pair of quavers:

238   Stravinsky: 1st Suite for small Orchestra, March

In this passage, where the trombones unfold a solemn *crescendo* and *decrescendo, legato* 'lightening' will do away with all clumsiness of motion and exaggeration of dynamic changes:

239   Brahms: IIIrd Symphony, 2nd Movement

The same device will impart to this rising melody in the muted trumpet (which might easily otherwise come out roughly) the barely perceptible onward urge which will save it from 'heaviness'.

240 Hindemith: Chamber-music No. 1, 2nd Movement

Avoiding a dropping of the tone.

If the tone is never allowed to drop, motif, melody and rhythm will always assume a definite evenness of tone. A pregnant instance of melodic consistency is afforded by the following rigid statement of the theme in augmented values by trombone and trumpet *ff*:

241 Reger: Symphonic Prologue

The same applies to this solo of the bass tuba:

242 Honegger: 'Pacific 231'

And to the great passage for trombones in Beethoven's Choral Symphony:

243 Beethoven: IXth Symphony, 4th Movement

In example 219 the horns, by not dropping the tone, will likewise achieve constancy of level in giving out the motif: the bass tuba will do the same in this *Ostinato* with every note underlined *marcato*:

244 Honegger: Pacific 231

111

In the following example from 'Till Eulenspiegel', consistency of rhythm is achieved by the same means, in combination with breathing with the attack, in the fanfare-like reiteration of one note:

245   Strauss: 'Till Eulenspiegel'

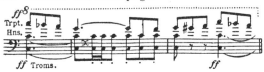

in the two crotchets in the 'Ruy Blas' Overture, which must be equally accented (but performed only *f*, not *ff*):

246   Mendelssohn: Ruy Blas Overture

and in this rhythm, which makes a sudden interruption and then drives onwards afresh, striving towards the close:

247   Beethoven: IVth Symphony, 1st Movement

Expressive motifs that on account of their technical difficulty of execution might wrongly induce 'lightening', and whose melodic course is in itself a falling off of tone, will be given firmness of texture and singing expressiveness if dropping the tone is carefully avoided:

248   Toch: Piano Concerto, 2nd Movement

This twofold impetus of the brass, which at the beginning of the Finale of Beethoven's Seventh Symphony comes as an anticipation of the *sforzandi* in the melody, calls for the same precaution:

112

249   Beethoven: VIIth Symphony, 4th Movement

(Note the tension-*crescendos*.)

It is particularly important not to drop the tone in the lower octave in low-pitched melodies given out by the brass; it is the only way of achieving the requisite expressive sonority not only in this lower octave, but throughout:

250   Strauss: 'Till Eulenspiegel'

Avoiding wrong crescendi.

Wrong *crescendi*, which should be avoided, tend to appear at the end of passages ascending to the apex of melodies:

251   Reger: Symphonic Prologue

when a melody moves upwards expressively:

252   Toch: Piano Concerto, 3rd Movement

when the motion proceeds to its climax upwards by consecutive degrees:

253   Busoni: 'Turandot', No. 2

(Note that in all these three cases (251–3) there is a tension-*crescendo* but no dynamic *crescendo*.)

113

and when a rise of the melody coincides with exposed registers:

254   Wagner: Meistersinger Overture

(Wagner writes the *p* at the entry of the horn only; therefore the melody of the first violins must be louder than the horn; the first violins must take the degree of *p* which the horn can achieve here as basis for their own degree of loudness.)

Extension.

Extension may be resorted to, for achieving an even, compact *legato ff* (see Ex. 241); to bring out a motif in *legato* playing:

255   Reger: Symphonic Prologue

to spread out a melody well—in association with a *crescendo* before a climax:

256   Reger: Symphonic Prologue

to carry through and steadily to increase a *crescendo* built up on a repeated motif:

257   Wagner: Meistersinger Overture

to bring out the difference between a stereotyped, persistently recurring *leggiero* pattern and a contrasted clumsy pattern:

114

258   Stravinsky: 1st Suite for small Orchestra, Polka

Listening while playing.

To listen while playing is one of the most universal requirements of modern orchestral playing. Leaving aside its fundamental importance, I shall give a few examples of problems which cannot be solved except by listening while playing.

In the Allegretto of Beethoven's Seventh Symphony, while the clarinets and bassoon are giving out the melody in A major, the trumpets (and flutes) come in *p* with four bars *crescendo,* the function of which is to lend a tender glowing colour effect. The degree of the *crescendo* depends entirely upon the singing strength of the melody, which must thereby receive additional luminosity and, in a measure, inner warmth; for this particular *crescendo* is no *espressivo* swelling-out, but is meant to accompany and support the onward urge of the melody.

In the Pastoral Symphony, the trombones have to impart brilliancy and breadth to an onward urge in a different way. Their entry must be adjusted by listening, and should come as a soft, final touch of light, a climax coinciding with the ringing sonority of the harmonic seventh, B flat:

259   Beethoven: Pastoral Symphony, Finale

Solo-playing and accompaniment—even when following upon one another as abruptly as in the next example—must be differentiated in both intensity and volume:

260   Reger: Symphonic Prologue

In the next example, where melody and accompaniment have notes of the same length, the horn-players must listen attentively, and comply with the barely perceptible extensions in the melody.

261   Mozart: Jupiter Symphony, 3rd Movement

The following passage in Brahms's 'Tragic Overture' with its even flow of melody unfolding over the sombre, motionless pedal of the tuba, also calls for independent listening:

262   Brahms: Tragic Overture

When it happens that one single instrument has to pass on from solo-playing to accompaniment or *vice versa*, the distinction becomes specially important:

263   Beethoven: IXth Symphony, Adagio

In order to ensure clarity in polyphonic developments built on motifs, let motif periods and accompaniment periods be well differentiated:

264   Honegger: 'Pacific 231'

116

The following passage in the Pastoral Symphony shows the difficulty of ensuring that a melodic line consisting of separate motifs given out by various instruments and in various registers shall retain its full structural value

265   Beethoven: Pastoral Symphony, Finale

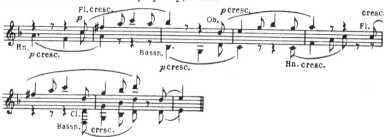

Here, the natural loudnesses, &c., of the instruments (notice the dull, weaker bassoon in the third bar) must be carefully calculated; and the actual *crescendo* must start with the fifth bar only.

In the next example, care should be taken that the trumpet entering in its vigorous middle register should, by moderating its tone, adjust itself to the horns, which cannot produce so full a tone in the foregoing high notes:

266   Honegger: 'Pacific 231'

The horn must proceed very cautiously in following the *crescendo* of the clarinet after this latter instrument has taken up the melody; it must increase its tone to a lesser degree than the lighter woodwind.

267   Schubert: B minor Symphony, 2nd Movement

Instruments that are different in loudness and lightness—such as the

117

trumpet and the flute in the next example—must carefully adjust themselves to one another (which is done by attentive listening): note that the
composer has given the trumpet *staccato* notes, and used rests.

268   Busoni: 'Turandot', No 2

In the soft passage for woodwind at the beginning of the second movement of Brahms's Third Symphony (in the light middle registers, with
equally limited contributions from the strings), there are cadential
phrases, *crescendo* and *decrescendo*, in which the horns must remain soft
and subordinate, barely indicating a swelling of their tone.

Here, the group formed by the clarinets and bassoons on one side and
the trombones on the other must be made to reinforce and complete each
other. This can only be achieved by means of careful and continuous
listening on both sides:

269   Schubert: B minor Symphony, 1st Movement

This is even more important when a passage is being passed from one
group of instruments to another, the music at the same time requiring
an even *diminuendo* from *ff* to *pp*.

270   Beethoven: 'The Battle of Vittoria'

Passing on a phrase.

This is a valuable resource when technical difficulties have to be overcome. It may occur in a melody:

118

271 Liszt: Dante Symphony

272 Honegger: 'Pacific 231'

Or melody and accompaniment merge into one another:

273 Beethoven: Pastoral Symphony, 1st Movement

(The triplets must be absolutely even, without any accents or break.)

274 Strauss: 'Till Eulenspiegel'

(The timpani notes must not be accented as if they were syncopated.)

275 Busoni: 'Turandot', No. 1

(Here, on the one hand, the theme must be well hammered out, and on the other an unbroken, even hammering of quavers must be obtained.)

276 Berg: Chamber-concerto for Violin and Piano

119

(Here the horns tend to enter too soon with their upbeats, and the trumpets too late with theirs, despite the precaution taken by the composer in providing the trumpet part with indications to obviate this.)

In the following passages the *rhythm* must be very accurately passed on:

277   Schubert: C major Symphony, 3rd Movement

278   Brahms: IIIrd Symphony, 4th Movement

If in example 278 the opposed rhythms, which are mutually stimulating, are accurately carried to their culmination, the *crescendo* power inherent in such rhythmic *agitatos* will become manifest.

When motifs are passed on between several instruments, it is usually because the whole passage would be technically impossible to play on one alone.

279   Bruckner: IXth Symphony, Scherzo

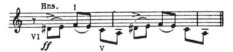

280   Honegger: 'Pacific 231'

The onward urge.

The correct determination and achievement of this onward impetus is the whole secret of a good performance. This kind of impetus is felt in *crescendo* passages.

120

281   Reger: Symphonic Prologue

(Usually, in this passage, the wind-instruments rise too speedily, providing a wrong and premature climax.)

In the unfolding of a melody to its main point:

282   Reger: Symphonic Prologue

In the immanent striving of a rhythm towards its end:

283   Toch: Piano Concerto, end of 1st Movement

In the intensification of repeated accents marking period-divisions:

284   Liszt: Dante Symphony, 1st Movement

In a polyphonic progression tending towards a general climax:

285   Tiessen: 'Prelude to a Drama of Revolution'

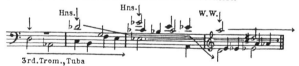

And in the persistent repetition of the same aggressive figure:

286   Beethoven: VIIth Symphony, 4th Movement

121

Muting.

A passage like the following, for muted brass quartet, is very difficult; but its beauty when perfectly carried out is ample compensation. The decisive factor is perfectly true pitch in the first chord. And even more vital is the perfect accuracy of all the different intervals that follow (in the first trumpet: major second and minor third; in the second, two consecutive major seconds; in the third, major third and minor second; in the tuba, minor second and major second). The difficulty is increased by the fact that the second half of the passage consists of exactly the same intervals in reversed order, and in the opposite direction. Moreover, all the notes must be played in quite even *pp* and perfect *legato*: hence it is easy to appreciate both the difficulty and the educational value of this passage.

287   Reger: Symphonic Prologue

In the next examples there is, on the one hand, difficulty in the second and first horn parts:

288   Reger: Symphonic Prologue

and, on the other hand, in the conspicuous seventh attacked by the fourth horn and the fading suspension in the third:

289   Reger: Symphonic Prologue

Equal volume of all notes in chords.

A very significant colour effect can be achieved by giving all notes of a chord perfect equality.

122

290   Reger: Symphonic Prologue

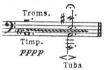

(If trombones and tuba play this final entry of theirs with their tone perfectly adjusted one to another, the effect will be approximately that of the rich, sombre pedal tone of the organ.)

291   Webern: Op. 6 (Orchestral Pieces), No. 4

If all the notes of this chord are attacked equally softly, and played with absolutely equal strength, the result will produce the illusion of a new, faintly sighing percussion instrument.

In the next example, it is only if the notes are flawlessly intoned and their volume perfectly balanced that the inner relationship (the harmonic gesture of the C tending to push on forwards from the restful, immobile fourth, F sharp–B) will be made clear:

292   Berg: Chamber Concerto for Violin and Piano

This cadence, in Bruckner's Ninth Symphony, also calls for absolute purity of intonation and perfect equality of volume of all the harmonic notes, so that the impetus of the deceptive cadence be directly perceived:

293   Bruckner: IXth Symphony, Adagio

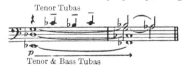

In the next example, the first horn must give out the C sharp cleanly and accurately, without nervousness (so that the discord be definite), and give it a volume equal to that of the D in the bass:

294   Toch: Piano Concerto, 2nd Movement

In Liszt's Dante Symphony the sonority of all four parts of the trombone-tuba quartet must be solemn, silvery, and of an easy mobility. Let the other three regulate their volume according to that of the first, the leader, and gently 'lighten':

295   Liszt: Dante Symphony

Grouping of instruments.

According to its grouping, an instrument may suddenly have to change its functions: for instance in the next example the horns, at first, provide a soft faintly metallic gleam over the darker tone of the woodwind (let the *crescendo* be well husbanded); but when the climax is reached they sing out freely, in their full capacity as pure brass instruments:

296   Beethoven: Pastoral Symphony, Finale

A model example of grouping is the great final melody in Reger's

'Symphonic Prologue' (beginning with the *Andante Sostenuto*, p. 122 in Peters' miniature score). The first four bars rely on the string timbre entirely; so that the associated bassoons can never play too gently. With the fifth bar, the woodwind comes to the fore, and the brass associated with them must keep to a bare minimum while the accompanying strings, evenly progressing, merely carry the general *crescendo* farther. With the upbeat before the eighth bar, the brass gains the ascendancy and develops the growth of sound in all-conquering *crescendo* up to the *fff* climax (note the clangorous ending of the melody in the trumpets and trombones). Then, as in a foreshortened reflexion (the eight bars being reduced to four), the registers are gradually withdrawn *decrescendo* until, at the end, the string timbre only remains.

This most instructive passage is worthy of very careful study. Any musician endowed with imagination capable of fully detecting the composer's intentions will thereby learn many surprising and fundamental things—first and foremost, he will learn much about Reger himself, suddenly realizing that his scoring never admits of retouching, but calls for style of presentment different from that which we usually apply owing to our training in classical and post-classical symphonic music.

PERFORMANCE AND INTERPRETATIVE POSSIBILITIES

Signs of interpretation.

There is no need to go into further particulars. Let it be remembered, once for all, that all that the composer stipulates in his dynamic and other signs of interpretation must be carried out; for instance, in Beethoven's Seventh Symphony, the *ff subito* (very often overlooked) of the whole orchestra when the Scherzo reappears, beginning *f*, and the sharp *marcati* that hammer out the canon in the octave in the last progression before the 'Court' scene in 'Till Eulenspiegel':

297   Strauss: 'Till Eulenspiegel'

Immanent laws which music must obey.

But whereas imagination detects the composer's conceptions and intentions, it must also acknowledge the unwritten laws to which the carrying out of these intentions is subject, and find practical ways of executing them in performance. For instance in the following melody, the horn should hardly start *f* as prescribed (it is playing in its best, naturally sonorous register); and the actual *crescendo* must take place in accordance with the increasing technical difficulties and obstacles to tone-expansion in the further course of the melody:

298   Berg: Chamber Concerto for Violin and Piano

In the second bar of Brahms's Third Symphony, the first and second horn must give out their third sonorously, for it constitutes the middle of the harmony of the diminished seventh into which the initial F major triad expands:

299   Brahms: IIIrd Symphony, Beginning

'Fulfilment' in performance.

As there is a method of teaching musical interpretation, so also ought there to be one for musical fulfilment—a curriculum whose object would be to complete all that has just been pointed out here for special purposes, and to organize it into a full survey of the possibilities of musical representation, setting forth the relationship between tone-conception and actualization, showing the obstacles in the way of a perfect concordance between the two, and the available possibilities of overcoming them; and, finally, subordinating technique to spirit and aiming at a presentation of the music that will coincide perfectly with the conception formed of it.

III. THE PERCUSSION

Use and significance of the percussion group.

Artistic music and the percussion instruments.

The great majority of percussion instruments give out notes of indeterminate pitch. Their sole function is to provide rhythms, accents, and tone-colours; only in a restricted way do they serve the artistic purposes of music proper. Nevertheless, to make them serve these purposes as fully as possible, to increase (without coarsening) their effectiveness by using them intelligently, calls for far greater attention to their technique than is at present the case.

Two groups: with and without definite pitch.

We shall begin with the instruments whose notes have a definite pitch —timpani, bells, gong, xylophone—and deal with the remainder (drums, cymbals, tamtam, triangle, tambourine, castanets) afterwards. But first let us make a few remarks which apply to the whole group.

The players.

Importance of technique.

The importance of a right technique of execution, and of quality of tone, is almost greater in the matter of the percussion than in the other components of the orchestra. A wrongly given out stroke of the cymbals sounds like a bang on a kettle and is a mere caricature of musical tone; the bass-drum, if not struck at the proper angle, sounds like toy explosions; tubes used in lieu of bells, if not struck exactly at the right spot, give out buzzing overtones instead of the intended note; the gong and the tamtam, if they do not vibrate isochronously to the end, have the effect of meaningless, merely external noises.

Percussion instruments are not 'accessory' instruments.

As often as not, all these instruments are played by musicians as sidelines; practically the only percussion specialists are timpanists, and sometimes players of the xylophone or of the side-drum. In consequence, not only are the subtler effects of the percussion disfigured, but the

127

instruments, in the hands of more or less occasional players, lose part of their accuracy and elasticity. One must either make a point of employing expert percussion players only, or take the trouble of rehearsing with the occasional players separately—which will soon show how very much makeshifts of this kind coarsen both the functions of the percussion and the works played.

The instruments and how to use them.

Quality of the instruments.

Even in good orchestras, instruments are sometimes found whose condition is appalling—antiquated timpani, the small one not high enough in pitch and the big one not deep enough, insufficiently resonant and affording no possibilities of shading; drums whose skins have lost their elasticity and toughness, all nice variations of sonority being thereby excluded; instead of separate pairs of Turkish and Chinese cymbals, only the one pair for both—although the difference in sonority between the two is definite, and both are to be used as required; instead of big bells a gallows of tubes, incomplete and perhaps out of tune with each other; and a triangle which gives out so many overtones that it seems to have a definite pitch comparable to that of a bell.

The timpanist, leader of the percussion.

The only person who can help the conductor in all these matters is the timpanist, as the leader of the group. He should see to it that all instruments be of good quality; that all timpani-players should have good sticks in sufficient variety; that if the score comprises a gong, a real gong (that is, a tamtam with a definite stipulated pitch) should be used; that drums of different sizes, with and without snares, a celesta, a Glockenspiel with keyboard and one without should be available. He should take care that the bass-drum be carefully brought to the degree of tension at which its tone is best, and loosened as soon as possible afterwards; and that the player in charge of it uses, intelligently, a variety of sticks and strokes, and never plays sitting; that according to the character of tone required, the gong and tamtam be struck in their centre or nearer the edge; and that according to the requirements of works played, higher or deeper gongs and tamtams be used.

Conductor, players, and timpanist.

Increasing difficulties of percussion playing.

The indefinitely pitched (properly non-musical) instruments are constantly gaining ground in modern music as carriers of accents and rhythms. Concurrently, the number of the problems confronting players has increased—by way of examples, I shall mention the handling of the percussion in Hauer's Seventh Suite and in Stravinsky's 'Les Noces'. But the players have not changed; they remain almost uninterested, they remain obstacles in the way of music. One of the many duties which the modern conductor has to face is to effect a transformation in them and in their playing.

The timpanist as the conductor's assistant.

The timpanist alone can help him. The first condition is that his own performance should be exemplary in the matter of ear, technique, and sense of responsibility. Further, he must be perfectly acquainted with and have mastered the technique of all the other percussion instruments, so as to be able, at all times, to direct and help their players.

1. INSTRUMENTS WITH DEFINITE PITCH

(a) *The Timpani.*

The timpani's part among percussion instruments is analogous to the timpanist's part among players. They are the most important and distinguished of the group, and afford the most valuable resources. They should be played, accordingly, with the skill that will utilize their extraordinary wealth of possibilities.

The sticks.

They are played by means of sticks which vary in three respects: the material they are made of, their size, and the hardness of their heads.

Material.

The material of which the heads are made generally determines the colour, power, and nuance of the tone. The usual types of heads are: felt-covered, flannel-covered, and cork-covered. The felt-covered give

129

the softest tones, the flannel-covered louder tones, more clearly detached from one another in quick successions; cork or wood heads produce hard tones, thunder-like in the *tremoli*.

Size.

The size of the sticks determines the volume of the tone. Big heads produce loud, clangorous tones; lighter, small heads soft tones. The players must be provided with sticks of each type with small, medium, and big heads. This will ensure the possibility of varying the volume of tone to the utmost.

Hardness.

Upon the hardness of the stick depend the nuances of tone. For each type and size of stick specially hard and specially soft patterns should be available besides the standard pattern.

Covering the range from pp *to* ff.

The range from *pp* to *ff*, as a rule, calls for the use of felt-covered sticks from *pp* to *mf* and of flannel-covered sticks from *f* to *ff*. Sticks with small felt heads are used for *pp marcato* beats, sticks with cork or wood heads for hard accents or clangorous rolls *ff*.

As shown, the timpanist has to command and differentiate an extraordinary amount of purely mechanical materials. Almost as varied are the processes of impact needful in order to put to use all these technical possibilities.

Point of impact.

Executing a roll crescendo.

The spot which the head must strike lies at a hand-breadth's distance from the rim. In the middle, the tone is less beautiful, duller, and also higher in pitch. A roll which has to rise to a climax is started near the rim whence the regular point of impact is gradually reached. In a *decrescendo*, the process is reversed.

Variants of the roll.

Other ways of carrying out a roll are possible: one stick may be striking the point of impact while the other is moved from the rim to this point; or different heads may be used simultaneously, at different spots and with different strengths. All these subtler possibilities have been used, so far, only in isolated cases. A rich field for experiment lies open to timpani-players who are interested in their instrument.

Style-characterization in the playing of the Timpani.

Use of light sticks.

Players of this kind will vary their sticks and methods according to the style of the works played. The music of Mozart and Haydn calls for light, chamber-music-like playing, which will simply bring out and underline rhythmic articulations, rolls crowning a climax, &c.

Medium playing.

Beethoven's symphonies call for a heavier and more richly varied mode of performance; likewise the music of the romantic composers and Brahms's four symphonies.

Use of heavy sticks.

In Wagner's music, all possible shades and degrees are requisite; but the mode of performance which characterizes his music is the heavy one, with the predominance of big clangorous tone.

Musical importance of the Timpani.

The art of the timpani-player consists in making plain, by his mode of performance, the musical significance of his part. His sensitiveness will enable him to decide how best to use in performance the natural difference in heaviness between his two arms:

300 Beethoven: VIIIth Symphony, 4th Movement

(The higher-pitched timpano is on the player's left, the lower-pitched on his right.)

301 Meyerbeer: 'The Prophet'

131

302 Meyerbeer: 'The Prophet'   303 Wagner: 'Rienzi'

304 Busoni: 'Turandot', No. 1

(b) *Bells, Celesta, Gong, and Xylophone.*

Deep bell notes are given out on tubes or bars, high ones on the glockenspiel with or without keyboard. When the tubes or bars are hung on their frame, care should be taken that the point of impact be easy to reach. And this point should be carefully determined in advance, because unless the right spot is struck, deep pitched notes will be accompanied by disturbing overtones.

Glockenspiel with and without keyboard.

The glockenspiel with keyboard should be used only when definitely prescribed by the composer. It has more mobility than the plain glockenspiel, but is less rich from the point of view of dynamics and tone. With the plain glockenspiel, further variety is achieved by the use of different hammers, some made of hard wood and others of metal. Even the plates of the glockenspiel may be made in different strengths to achieve further differentiations.

The celesta.

This instrument is remarkable for the fullness of its tone. When new and well played, it makes itself heard even in the *tutti* of a big orchestra.

The gong.

The tone of the gong does not differ from that of the tamtam but is definite in pitch. Sometimes, unfortunately, the point is overlooked, and composers prescribe a gong when they obviously mean a tamtam. Special care should be taken not to use the one or the other indiscriminately.

The xylophone.

The remark that most orchestras own old, bad percussion instruments applies chiefly to the xylophone. Where this instrument is prescribed, its special tone should be brought out flawlessly and with virtuosity. The best solution would be for one of the players to set up as a xylophone virtuoso and keep his own instrument.

Stravinsky's 'Crotales'.

These instruments which Stravinsky introduces at the end of 'Les Noces' are brass disks equal in diameter and thickness to a Swiss five-franc piece (roughly, to an English double florin). The first examples were cast in Paris in 1918, according to his specification. The pitch of these is the thrice-accented C sharp and B respectively. The score of 'Les Noces' provides no indications as to the 'Crotales'.

2. INSTRUMENTS WITHOUT DEFINITE PITCH

(a) *Drums.*

The bass-drum.

The bass-drum, unlike the other drums, stands on its side, so that the skin is vertical. It must not be struck at right angles to the skin but with a downward, almost vertical, movement. It is important that the instrument, before being played, should always be brought to its best tone by the adjustment of the screws.

The three kinds of roll.

Rolls of the big drum may be carried out in three different ways, which produce different effects and should be resorted to in different circumstances: with the head and butt-end of the stick held by the middle and made to oscillate quickly; with a stick provided with a head at either end and used in the same way; or with a pair of felt-covered timpani sticks.

Side-drums.

These are provided with catgut snares which may be relaxed in order to achieve shades of tone. But this relaxation and the simultaneous slackening of the skin impedes the sonority, 'mutes' the drums.

(b) *Cymbals.*

Cymbals and cinelli.

Each orchestra should have both types—the Turkish, known as cymbals proper, and the Chinese, or cinelli. The cinelli, preferred in

133

military bands, give out a hissing, buzzing tone very different in quality and accenting properties from that of the smaller, more ringing and metallic Turkish cymbals.

Correct grip when striking the fixed cymbal.

If one cymbal is fixed on to the bass-drum, the player must be very careful to hold the striking cymbal properly, with the thumb and first finger only and by the strap, without the hand touching the bulging part of the disk. The impact must be sideways, so that the cymbals may vibrate freely to the end.

'Stopping' and 'muting'.

Here 'stopping' means suddenly putting an end to the sound. This, with the timpani and bass-drum, is done by touching the skin with the hand or the finger-tips; the cymbal-player does it by sharply pressing his cymbals against his body.

But 'muting', which reduces the volume and vibration (as naturally happens when drum-skins are relaxed), is achieved, as regards the timpani, by placing a handkerchief (in accordance with the prescription *coperto*) at the spot opposite the point of impact. Single beats on the side-drums can be muted and varied as follows: the left-hand stick should be rested on the skin and struck with the other stick; if it is struck near the left hand, the tone produced will be higher in pitch than if it is struck near the drum-skin.

'Stopping' being a very important point, the special sign (') is used; it is placed over notes to stipulate immediate stopping. Let it be placed carefully wherever needful in the percussion parts, so as to ensure that important notes of the timpani, bass-drum, tamtam, gong, and bells shall be stopped neither prematurely nor too late.

(c) *Tamtam, Triangle, Castanets, and Tambourine.*

The tamtam.

Tamtams exist in different sizes, giving out more or less high, though always indefinite, sounds. For special purposes, the intermingling tones of either high-pitched or low-pitched tamtam may be divided into lower and higher. To this end the surface of the hand is used for muting:

placed in the centre of the plate it will absorb the deeper vibrations, placed near the circumference it will moderate the higher vibrations. This example again shows how many differentiations, as yet unexploited, can be achieved on percussion instruments.

The triangle.

On the triangle, the range from *pp* to *ff* is covered thus: for the *pp*, *p*, and *mf*, the upper sides of the instrument are struck; the base is struck to achieve *f* or *ff*. Here again, by using a variety of metal rods for striking, nuances can be achieved. For special effects, wooden rods (drum-sticks) may be used.

Anticipations should be started by a lighter tap on the left side of the triangle, a tap on the right side being used for the accented beat.

The castanets.

The castanets and the tambourine, being national folk-instruments, seldom come to their own when played in orchestras. They are then in the hands of occasional players, and for this reason often produce almost comic effects, whereas they should contribute charm and enhancement.

305   Wagner: Bacchanal in 'Tannhäuser' (Paris Version)

The sudden entry of the viola motif (played by the violas and 'cellos) with the rhythm accentuated by the dry tone of the castanets, should prove much more exciting and forceful, rising as it does from an almost inaudible beginning to a powerful climax, than the first time this motif was heard. What actually happens, in most performances, is that the castanets stand for very little: often the very rhythm is imperfectly rendered and there is neither *pianissimo* tone nor clear-cut movement.

135

The tambourine.

This instrument affords a whole range of possibilities: rhythmic patterns can be performed with the knuckles or the finger-tips, and the skin may be struck either with the ball of the hand, the fist, or the knee. Quickly repeated quavers are performed with the thumb, which is wetted and then rubbed along the surface near the rim. This causes it to rebound. If the motion is quickened and the pressure increased, regular quick rolls may be achieved.

By shaking the instrument and thereby the small sheet-brass cymbals with which it is provided, charming effects may be achieved—a case in point is the gently rustling ethereal *pp* effect in the Arabian Dance in Tchaikovsky's 'Casse-Noisette' Suite.

The moral of the foregoing remarks is that nearly all percussion instruments have been insufficiently practised until now, that a quantity of new effects could be obtained from them, and that if they were used with more differentiations, their aesthetic value would become correspondingly greater.

The obstacles are the inferiority of the players and of the instruments in use; for, with the exception of timpani and timpanists, percussion instruments and their players have been considered, hitherto, far too much as mere accessories in orchestras. It is the conductor's own interest to spare no means of improving, training, and rendering fully worthy of musical art this ever increasingly important group.

The Percussion in Orchestral Playing.

Accents and period-divisions.

The percussion achieves phrasing by marking accents or by bringing out the important notes of a rhythm or motif. Its most primitive use is for accenting strong beats:

306 Beethoven: 'The Battle of Vittoria'

307 Beethoven: Vth Symphony, 4th Movement

308 Hindemith: Orchestral Concerto (Chamber-music No. 3), 4th Movement

By these means, the tenor of a motif can be made clear if not determined by the composer's indications.

309 Tiessen: 'Prelude to a Drama of Revolution'

(That the mode of performance given here is the right one is shown by the fact that the same passage occurs farther on, marked *f*, and there the *crescendi* marked by the composer express the forward impetus that our indications imply.)

310 Beethoven: IXth Symphony, Adagio

311 Reger: Symphonic Prologue

The articulation into periods of a longer motif or melodic structure cannot be achieved except by means of fresh attacks (that is, slight accentuations preceded by slight pauses) corresponding to the detachment produced by breathing in wind parts.

137

312   Honegger: 'Pacific 231'

313   Hindemith: Chamber-music No. 1, Movement 4

Accuracy of performance.

Special technical accuracy in performance often determines the musical sense of a passage. For instance, in the Scherzo of the Choral Symphony, when the theme is about to reappear *ff*, the exciting roll of the timpani in triplets ending in the sharp crotchets of the theme is never made quite intelligible. Slight accents on the first beat of both the bars

138

in question will—if the player is technically adequate to the task—give the passage its true meaning to the ear:

314   Beethoven: IXth Symphony, Scherzo

The following very difficult accenting entries cannot be performed correctly unless the bass-drum player 'hears' the whole passage and sings it to himself:

315   Honegger: 'Pacific 231'

The same applies to the following examples of entries, both of which must be heard and seized rather than waited for:

316   Liszt: Dante Symphony, 1st Movement

317   Strauss: 'Till Eulenspiegel'

In the 'Quasi Marcia Funebre' in Busoni's 'Turandot', the drummer, in order to perform correctly the *pp subito* which occurs later, must not

139

start his initial *p* too softly. Conversely, in the following passage, he must distinctly differentiate *p* from *pp*:

318   Busoni: 'Turandot', No. 2

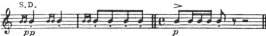

When there are technical difficulties in the way of instruments completing one another's contributions, these will be overcome by the players hearing the passage as a whole and making the required adjustments themselves. The entries of the percussion at the beginning of Kaminski's 'Magnificat' reveal the presence of such difficulties by the very indications with which they are provided. The natural tone-volumes of the various instruments differ, and yet the neutral *p* which is possible to all of them must be achieved. By the indications *p—ppp*, the composer gives approximations in view of the required common *p*.

The same applies to the following combination, which cannot be accurately conjoined unless performers listen most carefully while playing:

319   Busoni: 'Turandot',
        No. 8

The same problem occurs in another form in Webern's Six Orchestral Pieces. Perfect concordance between the muted trumpet and the faint duplicating notes of the glockenspiel is complicated by the difficulties of the slurs in the trumpet. Careful attention to the harp triplets may help to solve the problem.

320   Webern: Orchestral Pieces, Op. 6, No. 5

Playing in groups.

These remarks have brought us to group-playing, the first condition of which is that the activities of the players should be governed by their own listening. Usually, any forward impetus has to reach a dynamic climax, of which the reinforcement and crowning is taken up by other instruments. If the various participating instruments are unequal in natural volume, the strength of tone in performance must be adjusted accordingly by careful listening:

321 Reger: Symphonic Prologue

322 Toch: Piano Concerto, 3rd Movement

323 Stravinsky: 1st Suite, Galop   324 Kaminski: Magnificat, II

Similar adjustments may also be achieved by bringing the colour of an instrument belonging to another group as close as possible to that of the percussion. Here, for instance, flutter-tonguing in the trumpet part leads up to the roll of the side-drum:

325 Hindemith: Chamber-music No. 1, 1st Movement

141

Adjustment is a more delicate matter where motif or elements of similar order are given out by instruments which increase their tone simultaneously but are dynamically unequal. In the next example, the bass-drum covers the side-drum to the extent of masking its *agitato crescendi* in the first bar and the rhythm repeated in the first half of the second. The only way to bring these out is to moderate the *crescendi* of the bass-drum and achieve greater sharpness in the side-drum:

326   Tiessen: 'Prelude to a Drama of Revolution'

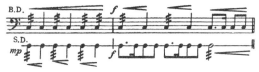

Relativity of dynamic prescriptions.

The relativity of dynamic prescriptions is clearly shown by the above examples. A few more will emphasize the point. In the next example, the *crescendo* prescribed for the timpani can express only the general dynamic motion. The timpani had better start actually swelling their tone with the fourth bar (parallel with the trombones and trumpets):

327   Reger: Symphonic Prologue

And even more relative is the following *crescendo-decrescendo*, which has to achieve a mere accompanying echo to the lightly gliding oboes:

328   Reger: Symphonic Prologue

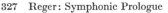

In Busoni's 'Turandot' Suite the glockenspiel, at first, should merely follow and support the woodwind in their *crescendo*; at the climax and conclusion in the third bar it should gain the ascendancy, rising *ff* to the high C:

329   Busoni: 'Turandot', No. 2

'Colours' of the tone.

The pedal-like entry of the final chord of the trombones and tuba in Reger's 'Symphonic Prologue' is preceded by a *crescendo-decrescendo* of the timpani. This the player should carry out most skilfully, so that the climax be exactly on the second crotchet and the decrease lead to and gently cover the entry of the brass:

330   Reger: Symphonic Prologue

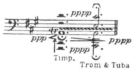

In the next example, the semiquavers of the glockenspiel must be full-toned and vibrating, so as to illuminate the whole orchestra. They must not sound hammered, but glide, *legato* and broadly, up and down the notes of the first inversion:

331   Busoni: 'Turandot', No. 2

The mysterious gentle pulsations (cymbals and bass-drum) in the first movement of the same suite should follow the rhythm of the timpani part, and be played with floating, gently stepping motion:

332   Busoni: 'Turandot', No. 1

The *tremolo* of the triangle in Liszt's 'Faust' Symphony must be played very softly and briskly, so as to suggest the effect of an indefinable hardly perceptible, soft silvery whirring accompaniment, rather than the actual instrument itself.

333   Liszt: Faust Symphony, 3rd Movement

The last note of the triangle in Kaminski's 'Magnificat' must be no more than a gleam of bright light gradually melting away. It is essential that it should enter without accentuation, sidling in unnoticeably, so to speak.

But in the next example, the timpani must not assert themselves as timpani: they must adjust themselves to the clear colour of the flutes, trumpets, and harps, and sound rather like a triangle, or better still, a silvery bell:

334   Busoni: 'Turandot', No. 5

In the *Adagio* of Beethoven's Choral Symphony, the soft notes of the timpani with which the one-bar motif, in inverted motion, retraces its

144

steps, must not only follow the retreating *decrescendo* but imaginatively carry to its end the soft singing tones of the wind-instruments (see Ex. 310).

'Stopping' and damping.

One example of stopping will suffice. In the next example, instead of the composer's express prescription 'stop quickly' we use the wedge-shaped sign (') which means the immediate stopping of the vibration.

335   Liszt: Faust Symphony, 3rd Movement

Damping, as an equivalent of muting, can be achieved, as a rule, only by the use of various hammers or rods. The next example calls for special sensitiveness of action; in order to 'get the feel' of the glockenspiel entry with its suitable volume and correct tone-character, the player must have a general conception of the effect of the points of colour of harp, viola, celesta, and flute in the melodic upbeat preceding his entry. Only thus will he find the shades of *pp decrescendo* suitable for his drooping, fading, answer.

336   Webern: Op. 10, No. 1

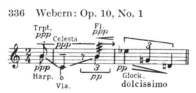

But the next pulsation of the glockenspiel must blend with the thrice-accented G of the solo-violin, merely adding almost imperceptible colour. The player should be provided with a special hammer; for he will hardly be able to achieve the prescribed *ppp* on this naturally clear high note of the instrument by merely altering his mode of striking. As regards the next example, an attempt must be made to increase the sonority of the *ff*

145

trills of glockenspiel (with additional *crescendo*) and of the entry of the triangle in trills *ff* and *crescendo* on the fourth beat, by using specially hard hammers and rods respectively:

337   Webern: Op. 10, No. 2

In the following nuances in the F sharps of the bell-rod (*ppp—pp—p—pp—ppp*) a mechanical means of carrying out the composer's prescriptions with greater ease should be resorted to—for instance, a less powerful, clearer-toned rod—especially for the last two notes.

338   Hindemith: Chamber-music No. 1, Adagio

As regards the soft, almost inaudible fading out of the third of Webern's Pieces, op. 10, care should be taken that the side-drum should not sound too clear (i.e. high). Otherwise, its entry, which should be unnoticeable, will produce the illusion of a reinforcement of sonority.

Correct playing of prescribed values.

Timpani-players often presume to alter repeated notes in short values into a continuous roll. The utmost accuracy should be insisted upon, because otherwise the effects aimed at by composers remain illusory.

146

Peculiar instruments in modern percussion.

In the last movement of Hindemith's Chamber Symphony a siren is used in the orchestra. At the end of Vogel's 'Sinfonia Fugata', a flexa-tone is included in the percussion. Both instruments are characterized by the fact that they produce, on account of the violent impetus given to their vibrations (by blowing and by quick shaking respectively), a tone that rises in pitch as it swells and then forthwith sinks and dies out. In order to ensure their effectiveness, their entry should be kept back until the last moment of the rush to the climax. If they start with a slow *crescendo* as prescribed, their tone is quite lost in that of the orchestra.

This leads us to the jazz band and to the lavish, ever-changing use of the percussion therein. Whatever one's own feelings respecting this modern branch of dance-music may be, one has to acknowledge that the clumsiest instruments of the orchestra have undergone a thorough revolution in the jazz bands. If one has once noticed how supple in their technique and independent in their musical functions the brass and percussion—hitherto the sheltered plants of the orchestra—have become in jazz music, one cannot help wishing that these new qualities could be utilized in concert orchestras, which should be ready to borrow technical stimuli and embellishments from the jazz band.

IV. THE HARP

The only instrument which we still have to deal with is the harp. For reasons of style, classics and romantics kept it out of the symphony orchestra. But they were not reluctant to use it occasionally, and they well knew how to utilize its special effects (as Beethoven does in his 'Prometheus'). But in the symphony orchestra, they sought to achieve harp-like effects in other ways. For instance, the accompanying anticipa-tory arpeggios of the strings in the *Adagio* of the Choral Symphony simply represent an imaginary harp in the orchestra, and have to be performed accordingly.

Special care should be taken that the harp be played so as to ensure that its notes will retain the same volume and force throughout its compass. There should be no weak registers in the harp. A quiet *glissando* should ring in the middle exactly as in the lower region; and in

147

the higher region, it should be as mellow as at the start. The same applies to scales and broken chords. An invariable rule is that passages of quick notes should never be 'lightened'.

When chords and single solo notes alternate, there should be no dynamic difference.

339   Beethoven: 'Prometheus', No. 5

Technical difficulties must never obtrude themselves on listeners; they should never be brought into prominence by rough, coarse playing:

340   Busoni: 'Turandot', No. 5

(no increase in loudness)

The following two passages from Beethoven's 'Prometheus' afford excellent material for study. Let them be used in order to acquire the art of achieving an absolutely even, smooth swelling or subsidence throughout a succession of notes:

341a   Beethoven: 'Prometheus', No. 5

341 b

Single deep notes which must stand out as solo notes or for purposes of articulation must be given their full force and their naturally bell-like tone:

342   Kaminski: Magnificat

But descending accompanying patterns must always be played comparatively lightly and softly:

343   Busoni: 'Turandot', No. 5

The next example calls for very accurate performance and careful adjustment by listening, so as to ensure the desired guitar-like evenness of the chords:

344   Casella: 'Italia'

When flute and harp follow one another as if forming one group, the dynamic standard is set by the flute, whose tone is more constant and has no pedal-like prolongations:

345   Beethoven: 'Prometheus', No. 5

In the following passage, it is very difficult to adjust exactly the loudness of the harp notes which twice (the second time as a self-echo) have

149

to take up from the concluding note of the downward gliding motif in the trumpet:

346   Webern: Op. 6 (Orchestral Pieces)

Marking the parts.

We have dwelt with especial care on the wind and percussion instruments, the two groups which hitherto were left to their own devices.

Conductors have either never been orchestral players themselves, or else have always been string players. For this reason they usually devote their most watchful attention to the strings, for which group they prescribe modes of execution in ever-increasing number. But the wind-instruments might profit by the conductor's help—not so much for unison group-play as for the solo passages which entail positive responsibilities.

When marking orchestral parts, it is needful to mark them all. Directions for execution are as important for the woodwind, brass, and percussion as for the strings. Hence, a conductor must have a thorough knowledge of every instrument in the orchestra, and of all the technical problems which the players may have to face.

The sole object of such marks is to enable players, by means of purely technical, explicit directions for performance, unmistakably to recognize and carry out the composer's ideal conceptions as clearly revealed in his score. These indications should not reflect a conductor's own 'readings', nor aim at underlining the conductor's individual view of the works. They are justifiable only so far as they contribute to the fullest possible exposition of the ideal of musical performance which was described on p. 17 above under 'clarity'.

Willem Mengelberg, the conductor of the Amsterdam Konzertgebouw Orchestra, uses such indications in exemplary fashion. I have seen string and choral parts used by him when conducting at the Frankfurt Museumgesellschaft, which fulfil their purpose in every respect. They do not enslave the players' individuality, but show the way to the best technical solution among the several that may be possible in every one of the cases that crop up.

150

CONDUCTOR AND MUSIC

A. THE TECHNIQUE OF CONDUCTING

THE most primitive way of 'conducting' consists in merely beating time. This may be done by audible counting or marking of the beats, and ensures that players will keep together. As the art of conducting progressed, visible representation of the metrical course replaced this audible guidance, and the perfect synchronism of the players, which had once been the only reason for conducting, has now come to be taken for granted.

There are three distinct purposes in conducting: (1) to present the metric course of the music; (2) to indicate its expressive, structural features; (3) actually to guide the orchestra—preventing faulty playing and correcting fluctuations or inequalities.

To present the metric course of the music is the basis of conducting. But the gestures which effect this presenting must simultaneously achieve the other two functions just mentioned. In conducting, a variety of artistic activities are united, and two opposite facets of genius are brought to bear—on the one hand the pure conception of musical works originating in the conductor's inner perception and intuition, on the other hand the critical and discerning watchfulness which has to mould the playing to this conception.

The Basic Types of conducting by gestures.

There are two fundamental types of gestures used in conducting, namely, a quick movement completed in the shortest possible time, and a movement long drawn out. These correspond to the two elementary opposites, *legato* and *staccato* (i.e. notes extended to a maximum and notes reduced to a minimum). Extended notes must be articulated into periods, *cantabile*; short notes must be organized rhythmically. The slow gestures presenting the melody, correspond to extended notes, and the quick gestures outlining rhythmic groups, to short notes.

We differentiate then, rhythm-forming abrupt conducting movements and melody-forming persuasive gestures. Rhythm-forming gesture marks the beginning of each time-unit and hastens straight on to the starting-point of the next gesture, which takes place when the time-unit referred to has run its course. Melody-forming gesture, on the contrary, starting with the time-unit, proceeds evenly, calmly, and continuously from the beginning of this unit to the starting-point of the next.

The beginning of Schubert's Second Symphony shows these two opposite types associated. The B flat major chord calls for rhythmic articulation; and while it continues sounding during the second half of the bar, being resolved simultaneously into a melodic pattern, melody-forming gesture comes into use.

347   Schubert: Symphony No. 2

The metric indication of the semiquavers in the first half is effected by short rhythmic gestures, from which, in the second half, the conductor passes on to broad, song-forming strokes:

This example was chosen precisely because it shows, at the very start of our theoretical disquisitions, how rhythmic and expressive gestures always go together. Let it be added that this contrast between the wood-wind giving out the chord rhythmically and the strings resolving this chord into melodic patterns shows the elementary basic antithesis between the groups of the orchestra.

Whole-bar, half-bar, triple-time, and quadruple-time beating.

The simplest example, and that which is the basis of all time beating, is the beating of a whole bar in one movement which is, as we know, characteristic of Beethoven's Scherzi. It consists in one movement first directed sharply downwards in a straight line, and then carried back straightway to its starting-point, to be repeated with the beginning of each bar.

Alla breve (2 in a bar) calls for the division of the above beat into halves. After the downbeat, the hand remains down until the end of the first time-unit, and with the beginning of the second time-unit rises back to the starting-point.

Alla breve beating must not swerve sidewards at its lowest point, but keep to the vertical line of 1 in a bar. Any swerving might prove ambiguous, because sideways motion characterizes the second beat in triple and quadruple time.

The following example shows the passing from 2 in a bar to 1 in a bar: the differentiation must be very accurate, so as to avoid uncertainty in the basses and 'celli:

348   Liszt: Dante Symphony

In triple-time beating the end of the first downward beat must at once

153

show its tendency towards further motion towards the right, and in quadruple its tendency towards the left:

The methods of beating 1, 2, 3, or 4 in a bar must be recognizable from the very first movement made. One cannot overstress the importance of the student's acquiring, by steadfast practice, an unambiguous method of carrying out these metric divisions best suited to his idiosyncrasies. Our object is to make possible a performance of a high artistic level, even when there has been no rehearsal at which mutual understanding between conductor and orchestra can be previously established. This can only be obtained by the perfect clarity and intelligibility of the conductor's indications of the metrical design.

In Liszt's Dante Symphony there are passages that show the transition from 2 in a bar to 4 in a bar. There the beating must be clear enough to preclude all possibility of mistakes on the players' part even if the time-signature is not marked in the parts:

349   Liszt: Dante Symphony

Four in a bar, three, two, and one (the last in 3/4 time) follow one another without transition in Schönberg's 'Chamber Symphony':

350 Schönberg: Chamber Symphony

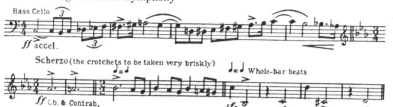

In order to acquire an absolutely clear execution of the various beats dealt with so far, the student should practise the following example:

351

Beating four, six, eight, nine, or twelve quavers.

When subdividing beats, binary or ternary (two crotchets into four quavers, three into six quavers, four into eight quavers, or two into six triplet quavers, and similarly three into nine and four into twelve), care should be taken that the main beats remain recognizable despite the subdivision. It is advisable not only to mark, slightly, the basic

155

movements, but also to indicate as an upbeat the last subdivisional value in each subdivided group:

In all subdivisional beating, care should be taken that the 'and' elements (as in *one* 'and' *two*, &c.) should be understood as continuations of the greater, basic motions, and that accordingly any new impetus should start only after these are completed (and never simultaneously), that is, when the next basic motion begins.

Preliminary upbeat.

The preliminary upbeat is the most important of all elements. It must determine the tempo quite unequivocally and correctly. It may be taken in two forms: firstly, to give the metronomic tempo, and secondly as a way of starting a phrase and partitioning a melody into periods. In the first form, its clarity is of decisive importance for beginning a movement or starting afresh after interruptions at rehearsal. In the second, as a means of expressing and representing, it is an indispensable element in the whole technique of conducting.

Executed clearly, it communicates unequivocally the tempo to the orchestra; so that if the pace remained the same throughout a piece, after the first downbeat no further indications should be needful. This point shows how very important it is for students to learn all that concerns preliminary upbeat movements. They should be made to consider the upbeat as determining the tempo of the beginning of pieces, and besides the tempo, the dynamism, the character of the entry, and the kind of playing required for this beginning.

The preliminary beat or upbeat must correspond to the metric units that follow and make their values recognizable. It should, therefore, be taken as follows—before a whole-bar *presto*, as a whole-bar beat:

352 Schubert: IInd Symphony

(It should be added that whole-bar upbeats preceding the beginning of pieces that start on the first beat of a bar must have a marked 'upbeat' tendency. Whereas for pieces that start with rests, whole-bar upbeats must be taken exactly as whole-bar beats, with the opposite tendency.) Before an *Alla breve-Allegro*, in the form of a second half-bar beat:

353 Mozart: 'Le Nozze de Figaro'

before the beginning of pieces in triple or quadruple time, in the form of the third, or fourth, beat, as the case may be.

354 Beethoven: IIIrd Symphony

355 Wagner: 'Meistersinger'

before an 8/8 *Adagio*, as for the eighth quaver of the bar:

356 Bruckner: IXth Symphony

These various upbeat motions must exactly correspond, in length and

157

direction, to the length and direction of the subsequent time-values which they represent.

Thus, in four-crotchet division, the upbeat will begin sideways and higher up than the *Alla breve* upbeat, which remains in line with the whole-bar beat; and in eight-quaver division the upbeat will start still higher up, and nearer the starting-point of the following downbeat than the four-crotchet division upbeat of which it is a subdivision.

The decisive factor in this upbeat is the will-power concentrated in it. When it begins, it must clearly say: '*Now* for the start; in this tempo, with such and such a *legato* or *staccato*; with this strength of *f* or softness of *p*, following my lead.' By the way it is taken, it must make every-thing quite clear and unequivocally perceptible to all the orchestra.

The upbeat-motions described so far refer to pieces beginning on the first accented beat. When a piece begins on the second accented beat (third crotchet in 4/4, fourth quaver in 6/8, &c.) the same principle applies: the preliminary upbeat corresponds to the second crotchet, or to the third quaver, &c.

357 Mozart: 'Eine kleine Nachtmusik' 358 Reger: Sinfonietta

But with works beginning on an unaccented part of the bar, the pre-liminary beat, which occurs where the accented beat would fall, and is, naturally, heavier, must be made a little lighter (preliminary beats before the second half of an *Alla breve*, before the second or fourth crotchet in 4/4, the second in 3/4, the fourth quaver in 6/8, &c.).

359 Beethoven: IXth Symphony

360   Haydn: E flat major Symphony

361   Beethoven: Great Fugue

362   Brahms: Ist Symphony

363   Brahms: Ist Symphony

364   Hindemith: Violin Concerto

365   Beethoven: IXth Symphony

366   Casella: 'Italia'

367   Wagner: Tristan Prelude

We must now deal with giving the preliminary upbeat when the beginning of a piece coincides neither with the strong nor with the weak part of the bar. There are many varieties of this occurrence.

(1) With the first bar written out in full:

368   Mendelssohn: 'Ruy Blas'

159

369   Stravinsky: 'Pulcinella'

370   Beethoven: IXth Symphony

371   Hindemith: Piano Concerto

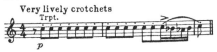

372   Reger: Symphonic Prologue

373   Schönberg: Op. 16, No. 4

374   Liszt: Faust Symphony

375   Strauss: 'Don Juan'

376   Mahler: IInd Symphony

377 Bruckner: VIIIth Symphony

378 Bruckner: IInd Symphony

The rule in such cases is: if the first bar is written in full but begins with a rest, no preliminary upbeat is made, and the conductor's first gesture signifies the beginning of this bar. Exceptions are made in cases such as examples 375 to 378, all characterized by the fact that notes occupy the greater part of the first time-unit, which starts with a rest. In order to ensure accuracy of performance here, let the conductor's left hand, raised to the height of the right hand ready for the downbeat, perform an accurate upbeat gesture. Then the right hand may start beating the '*one!*' of the bar as written, taking on from the left hand, so to speak, the preparatory upbeat which has tended towards it.

2. Beginnings before the first complete bar.

We encounter such beginnings consisting:

(*a*) of only one very small, partial metric value:

379 Mahler: 'Das Lied von der Erde'   380 Mozart: Overture, 'The Magic Flute'

381 Beethoven: Vth Symphony

382 Stravinsky: 'Pulcinella'   383 Mendelssohn: 'Ruy Blas'

161

Similar beginnings, but farther by one beat from the beginning of the first full bar, occur:

384   Beethoven: 'Prometheus'

385   Mozart: Sinfonia Concertante for Violins and Viola

(*b*) of two of these small partial metric values:

386   Weber: 'Oberon'

387   Haydn: G major Symphony   388   Mahler: IXth Symphony

(*c*) of three such values:

390   Mozart: 'Eine kleine Nachtmusik'

389   Mahler: Vth Symphony

391   Gluck: Overture, 'Iphigénie en Aulide'

In all such cases the same rule applies as was given under (1) above (first entries after the beginning of a fully written out bar); but instead of the fully written out bar, the conductor represents preliminary subdivisions by corresponding gestures. There is no preparatory upbeat. Again, notes may so encumber the initial rest (as happens in Exx. 390 and 391) that help in the form of an upbeat movement may be needful; this movement will be carried out as explained above, with the left hand.

As a general rule, the 'helping' upbeat of the left hand is to be used whenever the music does not begin on a beat and consists of more notes than are encompassed in one half of a beat. For instance, in example 391 the beat is a crotchet, and the *Grave* begins with three semiquavers. In example 390 the beat is a minim, and the beginning comprises three quavers. But in examples 379 and 380 the rest is far longer than the one note in the initial unit. In order to ensure an accurate entry, it is advisable to beat this unit as an upbeat with the right hand, and to mark the melodic pattern with the left moving upwards and meeting the right hand's downbeat.

The pause and the endbeat.

The upbeat fixes the tempo; its technique is used when a new tempo begins. Now for the use of the upbeat after a pause; for, even if the tempo remains the same, the resumption of movement has to be communicated to the orchestra.

We distinguish upbeats after a pause on a note, and upbeats after a pause on a rest.

A pause on a note may occur:

(a) immediately before the beginning of the next bar:

392   Mozart: Haffner Serenade

393   Beethoven: IXth Symphony

163

394 Beethoven: Vth Symphony

395 Beethoven: 'The Battle of Vittoria'

396 Beethoven: VIth Symphony

397 Strauss: 'Till Eulenspiegel'

398 Schumann: IVth Symphony

399 Schönberg: Op. 16, No. 2

400 Mahler: IIIrd Symphony

164

401 Reger: Symphonic Prologue

402 Reger: Symphonic Prologue

(*b*) at the beginning of, or within, a bar:

403 Beethoven: Violin Concerto

404 Beethoven: Great Fugue

405 Beethoven: VIIth Symphony

406 Beethoven: 'Prometheus'

407 Beethoven: VIIth Symphony

408 Beethoven: IVth Symphony

165

409 Beethoven: IIIrd Symphony

410 Casella: 'Italia'

411 Beethoven: Ist Symphony

412 Schumann: IVth Symphony

413 Mahler: IXth Symphony

414 Beethoven: Violin Concerto

415 Schönberg: Chamber Symphony

166

416   Beethoven: 'Prometheus'

417   Schönberg: Chamber Symphony

A pause on a rest can occur:

(a) at the end of a bar:

418   Weber: 'Euryanthe'

419   Haydn: E flat major Symphony

420   Haydn: E flat major Symphony

421   Stravinsky: 'Les Noces'

167

422 Beethoven: Great Fugue

423 Beethoven: IXth Symphony

424 Beethoven: IXth Symphony

425 Weber: 'Freischütz'

426 Beethoven: IXth Symphony

427 Wagner: Tristan Prelude

(*b*) at the beginning of, or within, a bar:

428   Cherubini: 'Ali Baba'

429   Weber: 'Freischütz'

430   Beethoven: 'Prometheus'

431   Casella: 'Italia'

432   Busoni: 'Turandot'

433   Beethoven: 'The Battle of Vittoria'

169

434   Beethoven: Great Fugue

Before dealing with the gestures to be used in all these examples we must consider the pause, as it occurs in all of them.

The pause—the extension of a note or rest beyond its metric value and for a practically indefinite duration—may occur in three forms:

(1) as the crowning extension of a note with full endbeat (or final pause);

(2) as the expansion, marking an articulation, of a note, with a halved upbeat (and as a pause preparing the sequel);

(3) as a prolongation with upbeat-like endbeat (without disjunction or rest).

The first case calls for the endbeat which we use for the ending of a piece—a motion characterized by the finality of the downward sweep which ends it:

The second case likewise calls for the endbeat, but directed sideways and indicating expectancy instead of being carried downwards to mark finality. The results will consist of interrupted period-divisions after the pauses—that is, additional new, pseudo-, rest-, or preparatory pauses.

(See Ex. 394 [the second pause], 397, 405, 416.)

In the third case the conclusive motion takes the opposite direction, and rises instead of ending with a fall. Here the negatory gesture simultaneously indicates the new upbeat:

(The pauses in Exx. 393, 395, 396, 399, 400 call for this motion.)

170

If we examine examples 392–434, we can see that, whenever notes or rests are extended by pauses after which the music immediately goes on, it is the third type of movement which has to be used. This applies to examples 392, 393, 394 (first pause), 395, 396, 398, 399, 400, 409, 410, 412.

The ending of a pause that becomes an upbeat must be a quick movement rising to the starting-point of the next downbeat, the point at which this downbeat will be expected.

But if a pause is followed by a break, the second type of movement must be used. This applies to examples 397, 403, 404, 405, 408, 411, 415, 417, 420, 421, 422, 423, 426, 428, 431, 432, 434.

A distinction must be made when the beat following the pause begins with a rest, and for this reason must not be preceded by an upbeat: examples 394 (second pause), 397, 405, 417, 421, 422, 426.

After the sideways ending of the pause-beat, the hand is to be kept at the point then reached—which is midway between the extreme points of the downbeat—during the break that follows; and from this point the movement is carried farther, in its normal direction, in accordance with the next unit (a unit beginning with a rest).

In example 403 we have, after the pause, an upbeat quaver. After the sideways pause-beat has ended at the midway point as explained above, and after the break, the conductor marks (at this height) the metric value of the whole second half of the bar, as if this half started with two quaver rests completing it.

In examples 404, 407, 408, 415, 420, 428, after the pause, the music moves on at once, no rest intervening; and small, upbeat-like impelling movements must precede and prepare this continuation. Here again, it is at the midway point that the moment to continue is awaited. The small, halved, impelling motion continues the movement of the concluding beat, in the same direction, as an echo of its energy; and the contrasting new motions that follow upon it are to be clearly connected with it.

Three of our examples call for special consideration. In examples 409 and 412, the upbeat-like conclusive motions coincide with the second time-unit so definitely as to become identified with it, and the upbeat-like conclusion becomes the second half of the bar. But in example 410 the duration of the pause is sustained by the raised left hand while the right hand, beating sideways, carries out the upbeat-like conclusive motion.

Pauses must be immediately recognizable. Therefore the arm that indicates them must be raised high and be clearly visible. This means that with pauses in the first half of a bar (see the above three examples) the right hand must carry the downbeat to its end, but immediately afterwards return to the midway point—revolving slowly in examples 409 and 412, but swinging back briskly in example 410:

Finally, let us consider examples 401 and 402, in both of which we have a pause at the beginning of a bar and further stoppages later on. Here, the raised left hand must determine the duration of the main pause, while the right hand quietly beats the units until the later stoppages are reached.

When the full end-beat has to be used—before repeats, between two sections, &c.—the pause on a rest at the end of a bar is not given, and it is on the last note before this rest that the conclusive pause-beat takes place (Exx. 418, 419, 424, 425, 427, 430, 433). Whether this last note before a pause occupies the first, second, or third beat of the bar does not matter: the normal movement corresponding to it must always be carried downwards at the finish, to mark conclusion:

Conclusion on 'two' in 3/4 time (Ex. 433).   Conclusion on 'three' in 4/4 time (Ex. 425).

Example 429 constitutes an exception in a way. The endbeat that ends the *ff* chord has to be carried out as a downbeat (first beat of the bar containing the pause). But from the lowest point of this downbeat, after the end of the pause, the second unit of the bar, beginning with a rest, starts forthwith, without any preparatory motion. Likewise, in example 434, the endbeat must follow upon 'two'.

There is one more case to consider. In example 432 the pause in the woodwind parts is placed over the fourth quaver-value; but in the string parts it comes in over the third (correctly written, it ought to stand over the seventh semiquaver value). Here, the first thing is to complete the conducting of the woodwind—that is, give them the first two crotchets. The second crotchet is started in the normal direction (as in the cases previously examined), but ended downwards and to the left by an anticipated conclusive pause-beat. A further upbeat to the left, in the direction taken by the beating of the second crotchet, precedes the entry of the strings. This upbeat is to be carried out as if the upbeat semiquaver of the strings was preceded by a dotted quaver rest.

General pauses and caesuras belong to the same category as pauses over rests. The former, indeed, corresponds to the cases examined above; but the technique of carrying out caesuras is more complex. A general pause can occur at any spot within a bar, whereas a caesura usually occurs on the junction of two bars. The functions of the general pause are to end, to mark an articulation, to prepare; but the caesura stands for a breathing, a final, quick gathering up of forces.

The General Pause.

The following examples show the variety of the ways in which general pauses may occur:

435 Weber: 'Beherrscher der Geister'

436 Miaskowsky: VIIth Symphony

437 Miaskowsky: VIIth Symphony

173

438   Miaskowsky: VIIth Symphony

There is nothing new to us in example 435: as before, the conclusion of the second pause (the pause on the rest) is shifted, so as to coincide with the downbeat ending the pause on the dotted semibreve; and it is only after the break-pause that the motion which prepares the next bar by means of an upbeat has to start.

In example 436 the second whole bar is to be beaten after the fashion of a conclusion, downwards; and thence the motion covering the general pause value is carried up to the starting-point of the downbeat that will follow this general pause, and it takes the form of an upbeat indicating the *sostenuto*.

In example 437 the transition from 2/2 to 3/4 (= a whole bar) is achieved by the general pauses. In the last 2/2 bar the beat of the second half must be an upbeat-like endbeat. The first general pause, which follows, is marked with a small normal movement; but the second must be beaten as a preparatory whole-bar beat, with an upward tendency.

In example 438, too, it is important to introduce endbeat and upbeat movements. The second whole bar must be given an upbeat-like endbeat (*quasi* 3/4 *plus* 3/4), the general pause that follows is only marked, and the next bar is beaten upwards as an upbeat. Then come: the downbeat ‖ ♪♪ ♩ ♩ ‖; two lightly marked whole-bar pauses; and, to prepare the downbeat ‖ ♩ ♪♪ ♩ ‖, the third general pause is beaten upbeat-wise.

The Caesura.

Caesuras are especially frequent in modern works. The caesura is an important point in musical performance; at times it must be resorted to even if not stipulated by the composer. It occurs under three forms:

174

(1) As a short general pause, indicated by a pause over the bar division:

439   Mahler: IIIrd Symphony

440   Mahler: IXth Symphony

441   Bruckner: IXth Symphony

442   Beethoven: IXth Symphony

(2) As a short breathing, a gathering-up before a fresh beginning, or as a break between two phrases (marked '):

443   Mahler: VIIIth Symphony

444   Strauss: 'Don Juan'

175

445   Schumann: 'Genoveva'

(3) As a means of clearly separating segments, different in character, but following one another without intervening rest; and, generally speaking, to mark divisions between periods where the composer indicates none:

446   Beethoven: IXth Symphony

447   Brahms: IIIrd Symphony

As regards example 439, it is advisable to shift the pause back by one crotchet-value—that is, to mark it between the third and fourth beat of the bar, so as to ensure a normal, effortless upbeat. Let the first three beats be carried out so that on 'three', the motion ends on the right, sideways and downwards. Then, wait for the time allotted to the pause, and start upbeatwise the movement corresponding to the fourth crotchet-value.

In example 440 the last beat before the pause on the bar-line must be carried out as an upbeat-endbeat of the third beat: the hand remains poised high for the duration of the caesura, until the moment comes for the downbeat, which follows without preparation.

Before the pause on the bar-line in example 441, the whole-bar beat must include a semi-endbeat on 'three'—more or less by way of endbeat to the second crotchet; after this, the right hand remains poised midway and then takes up the scherzo again with a direct downbeat.

176

In example 442 the last whole-bar beat before the pause must come as a conclusive motion following upon the beating of the previous bar; and afterwards the hand must remain poised midway. When the moment comes, the new tempo must be indicated by an accurate upbeat.

In example 443 the caesura must be preceded by an upbeat-endbeat bringing the hand to the spot at which it waits. The quavers of the triplet must be beaten singly. After the break, the downbeat follows without preparation. The same way of beating is used in example 444.

In example 445 the motion corresponding to the fourth crotchet ends in a downwards endbeat. The eighth quaver is to be beaten upwards without preparatory upbeat, the motion exactly equalling in duration a minim of the *allegro*.

In example 446 the *ff* chords of the orchestra preceding the 'Hymn to Joy' must have a definite conclusive tendency. Accordingly, the chord on 'three' must be beaten almost as a new 'one', with a conclusive motion arrested half-way—the upbeat preparing the *p* entry of the 'celli and basses to follow.

In example 447 the return of the strongly rhythmic motif which is part of the first theme of Brahms's Third Symphony, taking place as it does after a long rise to a climax, calls for a distinct marking of the coincidence of the upbeatwise ending on 'three' and upbeatwise beginning of the motif on 'five'. The intervening caesura on 'four' must be emphasized, in a measure, by a slight extension of the pause. To that effect, the first half of the bar must end with a sideways conclusive motion for the third crotchet; after a short wait, the second half of the bar is beaten with an emphatic, pushing, upward motion.

Pause and Caesura in the interpretation of Melody.

The last example shows how the technical processes of beating previously described are to be used in the course of the music. Before taking up a well-known score and submitting it to a systematic technical analysis, we have to deal with a few more particular cases.

The pause and the caesura may occur in the course of a melodic pattern, to indicate agogic extensions or divisions:

177

448 Mahler: IIIrd Symphony

449 Mahler: IIIrd Symphony

In both the above cases the left hand must come into use. In example 448 it will remain motionless at the spot at which the second 3/2 beat took place, while the right hand goes through the halved, upbeat sideways motion leading to the next pause. Both hands simultaneously reach the spot at which the third 3/2 beat—the second pause in the bar—takes place, and afterwards again carry out similar separate tasks. For here each hand has a distinct function: while the left merely marks the metric values of the 3/2 time, indicating them without ambiguity to those performers who have rests, the right represents the melodic significance as made clear by Mahler with the help of the pauses and caesuras. Of course, the upbeat motions that follow upon the two pauses must be started with a small, precise conclusive beat, so as to make sure that the cor anglais always marks the divisions correctly (even if the caesuras happen not to be marked in the part).

Example 449 gives us a problem to solve. We must remember that our uniform procedure is to deal with every case as if accurate indications for performance were lacking in the parts, and the correct fulfilment of the composer's intentions depended entirely upon the way in which the conductor indicated those intentions. The problem may therefore be solved as follows: the right hand again represents the inner melodic life of the cor anglais part—that is, the first pause is followed by an inserted upbeat preparing the second extension; and during this upbeat, the left hand, kept down after the downbeat, must very definitely sustain the first pause, moving upwards, towards the second pause, only after this inserted upbeat has run its course. Both arms mark the second halt, after which the left starts beating 'three' and 'four' sideways for the horn, and the right, simultaneously with the upward motion of the left on 'four', beats the same metric value as an upbeat for the final quavers of the cor anglais.

Uses of upbeat and endbeat movements.

Every tempo must be determined by an upbeat. Therefore, whenever a new *a tempo* follows upon a *ritardando* without a rest, the question arises, how will it be possible to indicate the new tempo by a precise upbeat despite, and within, the *ritardando* course of the music. There are two dissimilar cases:

(1) The simpler, when the change of tempo takes place at the beginning of a bar; and

(2) the rarer case, when the change occurs within a bar:

450   Reger: Symphonic Prologue

451   Reger: Serenade

In example 450 the six crotchets *ritenuto* must be beaten with movements steadily decreasing in amplitude; these must retain their normal direction, but in the second half of the bar, the central point of the beating must be brought slightly down. The beating of the sixth crotchet begins with the end of the *ritardando*, so that the upward motion has only a little way to go; then from this point the motion is carried on (as if in beating two separate quavers) to give the exact pace of the succeeding *a tempo* by an upbeat.

Whenever a *ritardando* and an *a tempo* follow directly upon one another,

179

the rule is that the last *ritardando* beat is to be divided into two movements, the first of which belongs to the *ritardando*, whereas the second determines the new tempo.

Likewise in example 451, in the bar in which the second violins enter, the fourth quaver must correspond to the third crotchet, which follows upon it: this means that in this bar, not only the third and fourth quavers must be beaten to the left as the two halves of the second crotchet beat, but that the upbeat motion for the fourth quaver must indicate the *grazioso* character of the *a tempo*.

In both our examples, apart from the contrast between *ritardando* and *a tempo*, the beating of the last *ritardando* quaver-value plays a decisive part, and must clearly mark the fundamental contrast between *legato* (singing) and *staccato* (rhythmically accented) types of music.

Motif upbeat.

We have not yet exhausted the question of the upbeat and endbeat movements: in fact, there is hardly a bar of music in which the conductor does not have to use variants of both. Let us now consider the motif upbeat:

452   Reger: Symphonic Prologue

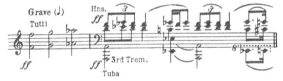

The triplets in the second bar are given out by three pairs of horns; and, coming as they do after the stiff *unisono* of the whole orchestra, they constitute a rhythmic expansion of chords which is important as regards the further course of the work. To give their entry at once sufficient substance and power and accurate definition, it is absolutely necessary to give the horns a conscious preparatory upbeat motion to go by.

Similarly (but for another purpose) the motif upbeat has to be used at the beginning of Honegger's 'Pacific 231'. At the second bar of this work begins a fourfold repetition of a rhythmic motif whose duration is six crotchets: this motif starts with a heavy thud in the double-basses *pizzicato* and muted horns, to which loud, hissing flageolet accents of the strings reply.

453   Honegger: 'Pacific 231'

In order to render the rhythmic structure clear, upbeat motions must precede both the *pizzicato* beat and the flageolet *sforzando*, whereas for the *decrescendo* after this *sforzando* the motion must almost cease—but of course, this 'cessation' must be relative, so as not to affect the clarity.

At the beginning of Busoni's 'Turandot' Suite we have the following very instructive passage:

454   Busoni: 'Turandot'

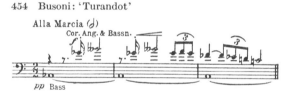

Twice the cor anglais and bassoon have to play upbeat semiquavers: the first time occurs immediately before the second half (minim) of the bar, but the second time the beginning of the motif is shifted to the second crotchet of the bar, with a resulting syncopation. In the first bar we must prevent starting the semiquaver too soon, and make it come, lightly and accurately, just before the second minim beat. But in the second bar the players, misled by false analogy, will tend to delay their entry. This must be avoided. Both these objects are achieved by corresponding ways of beating; in the first bar, the downbeat takes place normally, and the second beat is carried forcibly upwards, the left hand marking the semiquaver upbeat preceding it; but in the second bar, the downbeat must be taken swiftly and firmly, so as to draw the parallel motif towards the beginning of the bar, so to speak.

181

In the first theme of Brahms's Third Symphony, the second half of each of the first four bars must be given distinct accented movements. In order to make clear the structure of the motif-portions in these bars, these second dotted minims must be conducted as impelling motif upbeats:

455   Brahms: IIIrd Symphony

Motif endbeat.

In Beethoven's 'Coriolan' overture there are two passages for which the motif endbeat must be used:

456   Beethoven: 'Coriolan'

457   Beethoven: 'Coriolan'

Both these end on the weak beat of the bar, the ending being emphasized by a f chord of the wind-instruments. In order to achieve the desired effect, example 456 is to be conducted as follows: in the second bar, the downbeat of the right hand is made with a slightly sideways movement, and is held on, the following minim value is taken in the same direction, and for the fourth crotchet comes an upbeat-like endbeat, an upward motion. During the first three beats the left hand is held down motionless, but on 'four' is used jointly with the right to reinforce the endbeat in upward motion.

In example 457 the process is the same, except that after the upward beat in the first bar, the left hand remains poised, and is brought down only on the second crotchet of the second bar, whereas the right hand divides the first minim of the second bar and, after falling on 'one', gives a downward endbeat for the second crotchet.

There are motif endbeats in the Choral Symphony:

458   Beethoven: IXth Symphony

For both these *f* chords on 'three', upbeat-like endbeats have to be used.

Period-division by means of upbeats and endbeats.

When a melodic curve is formed by coupled motifs which no definite break separates, upbeat and endbeat motions are required in order to render the concealed structure clear. Many such cases occur in Reger's music, in which endings and fresh starts are often intertwined in a way which, quite apart from the skill required to solve the technical difficulties which they represent, call for uncommonly sensitive musicianship on the conductor's part—otherwise the music will come out formless and viscid. Here are instances from the 'Symphonic Prologue':

459   Reger: Symphonic Prologue

460   Reger: Symphonic Prologue

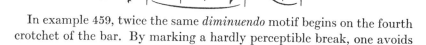

In example 459, twice the same *diminuendo* motif begins on the fourth crotchet of the bar. By marking a hardly perceptible break, one avoids the danger of the entry of the horns remaining too closely connected with the preceding half of the bar. The same applies to the entry of the strings in the third bar: both times, at the boundary between 'three' and 'four', the music must die away so as to mark a slight interruption.

The technical process to be applied to these passages consists in reducing the amplitude of the motions in the first half of the second bar, the left hand remaining motionless from the start of the dotted minim, and in marking a barely perceptible stop on the third subdividing beat of the right, to await the syncopated quaver. After this, the right hand performs another light quaver motion without swerving from the direction in which the third crotchet was beaten, and then beats the fourth crotchet for the horn entry by means of a distinct motion to the right. This provides a rest-like extension inserted before the second entry of the motif; and the need for a similar extension before the entry of the strings is even more pressing.

Example 460 is dealt with similarly. Here, two groups of instruments intertwine motifs (given out *diminuendo*) so as to form periods embracing two bars and a half. The horn theme is to be taken with slight *ritenuto* extensions in the second half of the first bar. The last crotchet of the answering bass motif must end even more quietly, and die out. Again the third crotchet is given an imperceptible check (third bar, before the beginning of the second period of two bars and a half), and a slight upbeat quaver motion is inserted, in the direction of the third crotchet beat, so as to mark the articulation.

In the next example, correct performance can be ensured only if the normal whole-bar beats are constantly transformed into upbeat or end-beat motions:

461   Reger: Sinfonietta

The third, seventh, tenth, eleventh, and twelfth bars call for downward endbeats. Conversely, the second, sixth, and ninth call for upbeats. In the third bar, the third, accented quaver must be marked by the left hand. It is difficult to perform correctly the threefold rise to the B flat, the approach to which occupies two bars, then three, and then again two. The required power depends entirely upon the *crescendi* leading up to each conclusion. The third rise, embodying the final conclusion begins (eighth bar) as an upbeat in order to reinforce the driving-power.

The next example shows, principally, articulation by means of endbeats:

462   Reger: Sinfonietta

This melodic structure clearly means one thing: singing and *diminuendo* to the end. At the second and sixth bars, it dies out so completely that all movement has to be arrested—the break taking place both times on the third quaver; after this extension, the fourth quaver, taken with an upbeat motif, leads on to the sequel. But in the fourth bar there is no break: *decrescendo* and *crescendo* are so closely intertwined, that the dying-out motion revives immediately as an upbeat.

We have dealt, so far, with the elementary gestures. A few examples have shown certain applications of these, so that the two categories, purely metrical indication and expressive, formulative presentment, soon commingled. However, we restricted ourselves to particular cases, so as to face clearly defined problems. The next part 'The applied technique, or practice, of Conducting', will show how these elementary gestures are to be connected with one another and used on living works; and it will lead students to determine practical cases in which a third function comes into being—a critical, piloting function, the conductor smoothing the players' way, foreseeing everything from both the technical and the intuitive point of view, and carrying out necessary changes in advance. In short, we shall be dealing with actual conducting and with the ideal towards which the practice must strive. But before this we have still a few principles to set forth.

The natural starting-point of the motions of Conducting.

All the advice given in this book for the technical solution of definite problems sets forth single tested possibilities of satisfactory execution. Carefully studied, it will safely lead the student to the point at which, by thoroughly studying cases as they occur, he will speedily discover the modifications that correspond to his own individuality.

The natural starting-point of all conducting motions is that where the fingers come to rest when the right arm, half extended, is raised forwards, shoulder-high. This raising naturally results in a slight curve of the elbow, which curve is restricted by the fact that when the arm moves thus, the elbow is slightly raised sideways and to the right. This position makes possible the performance of motions upwards, downwards, away from the body or towards it, and sideways to the right or left. Motions downwards, to the left or right, and upwards, are to be used exclusively for indicating the metre; but when they are brought closer to or farther away from the body, they acquire a power for expressive presentment. Unconsciously, we associate the notion of greater volume of tone with larger gestures, and that of a decreasing volume with a decrease of their compass. Hence the rule for indicating f or p, *crescendo* and *decrescendo*: motions that start from the natural starting-point and revert to it indicate the most neutral type of volume and intensity, that is, the *mf*. For a *crescendo*, the motions not only increase in amplitude, but their starting-point is carried farther forwards, away from the body. Conversely in p, not only are the gestures smaller, but the starting-point is brought closer to the body.

All this shows how wide a diversity of combinations are available. It is the conductor's sensitiveness and his capacity to conceive clearly and thoroughly that will enable him to use them all discriminatingly and always unambiguously.

186

A way of 'extinguishing' sonority is to bring the motion quite close to the body. Conversely, the amplest and most concentrated gestures must be reserved for dynamic and expressive culminations. It is therefore important always to keep in mind the neutral centre of tone-volume and of amplitude of gesture, and most carefully to proceed thence in the one direction or the other. And especially one should try to keep in reserve, in their unimpaired freshness, the most intensified or reduced gestures for the extreme points to which they correspond.

The Conductor's Bearing.

Conducting should never be confused either with dramatic acting, pantomimic presentment, or gymnastics. Its ideal should be that no part of the body except the right arm should move. There is no need to resort to distorting emotional grimaces; on the contrary, the eyes should be kept quite free, alert, and ready, for they must watch, help, indicate, and encourage the players, and keep the conductor in touch with every one of them.

If all the rest of the body keeps in repose, attention is automatically restricted to the right arm, to which all movement is practically confined. A natural, easy, fixed position of the feet will prevent the lower part of the body from moving. So far as possible, all needless bending of the body should be avoided. But one should likewise avoid tension, and the rigid repression of slight automatic movements of the body. Just as the head turns towards the various players as the conductor looks at them, so does the body slightly follow the gestures. But all this must be kept down to a minimum, and take place easily, unconstrainedly. It is only if a conductor is altogether free from constraint, and if his controlling energies are never cramped or distorted, that he is capable of carrying his orchestra to the utmost development of its power and getting the best from each player.

In any case let the student avoid the duplicating, simultaneous use of both arms, which never renders his motions clearer for the orchestra, more expressive, or more relevant. On the contrary, the practice robs a conductor of an important resource as regards expressive, representative conducting. When it remains independent of the right arm's motions (but still employing the unambiguous, basic metrical signs) the use

187

of the left hand is a splendid method of articulating, intensifying, reinforcing, emphasizing, hushing, and refining. Hence, the proper and differentiated use of the left hand in conducting (during the use of the right) will have to be dealt with more thoroughly in the next section.

Clarity of conducting motions.

By way of conclusion, I beg leave to repeat that all the prescriptions in this book refer to the cases in which conductor and orchestra meet without previous acquaintanceship with one another, or previous rehearsal for the purpose of mutual understanding. The object must remain perfect clarity of presentment—an unambiguity of gesture that will exclude all possibility of doubt. Even if the orchestral parts were devoid of indications the conductor's gestures should make easily and compellingly clear all points of dynamics, pace, quality, and degree of expression at every moment of the music.

The conductor must carry the whole of the work in his head, and thoroughly achieve the visible presentment of his conception. The ease and freedom with which he makes himself the carrier of the work communicate themselves to the players, who in turn are thus enabled to master without effort the matter they handle.

Conducting is a contact between human beings. The more simple, clear, and concentrated the contact is made, the more intelligible and telling its effect will be; and thus the players will be able, all the more joyously and enthusiastically, to allow the music to become a real work of art.

B. THE APPLIED TECHNIQUE, OR PRACTICE, OF CONDUCTING

WHEN a student confronts an orchestra for the first time, he must have thoroughly mastered the practice of his craft. He must be not merely theoretically able to conduct an orchestra, but actually capable of dealing with the realities of the orchestra. It is not enough that he should be able to represent his ideal conceptions of works unambiguously and with infectious intensity: he must add to this capacity that of leading the orchestra so as, in the course of playing, forthwith to correct faults, to help through special difficulties, to adjust the balance in advance—in short, to establish a reciprocal relationship between conception and actual performance.

This is the part of conducting that proves most difficult to learn, the mastery of which is the only justification of the name of 'conductor'. The question is, how can practice be acquired without practice? How is the student to learn to overcome the technical problems of conducting without having an instrument upon which to practise? The only solution is for the teacher to represent this instrument; to play the part in turn of the intelligent and attentive player and the uninterested, reluctant player, varying in quality and in willingness, as actually occurs in orchestras. With his teacher, the student must experience all the cases that occur in practice; and in front of his mirror, he must find the way of studying and controlling his technique on his own. Before ever beginning to conduct, he must learn that if the orchestra goes wrong under his guidance, the fault lies with him. Therefore, his own contribution can never reach a high enough level; even when conductor and players co-operate with one another finely and sensitively, there is always room for an even clearer presentment and for an easier mastery of subject-matter.

Conditions of teaching.

Here is a method of tuition by which it will be possible to bring the student, in a comparatively short time, to a clear knowledge and command of the problems of conducting.

The first conditions are great and keen musicianship; a keen sense of hearing and a capacity to differentiate every component part of what is heard; and a power of imagination which will bring music to intense inward realization without the help of any instrument. Further, the student must know all about the forms and technical resources of composition. He must be capable of making out rhythmic, melodic, and harmonic analyses of musical works. But, first and foremost, he must be naturally endowed with the capacity (which can be accurately tested after a very few hours of study) to translate clearly and intensely, by his conducting motions, his vivid conception of a work.

The alpha and omega of conducting is the capacity to conceive an absolutely ideal performance in the imagination. Failing this, even the most outstanding manual capacity is of no value, and a conductor will be, at best, a skilful time-beater.

As to the imaginative capacity ('hearing what one sees') no more will be said here, for it is indeed the fundamental requisite for *every* kind of musical study. Failing it, music, instead of being the most human of all art-practices, is merely a possibility of manipulating an instrument. But the importance of ideal conceptions has been emphasized repeatedly in the previous chapters of this book, for the particular reason that the conductor, who is merely a spiritual intermediary, stands in far greater need of this fundamental power than any other musician.

Method of tuition.

Let the student and the teacher face one another as conductor and orchestra. At first the teacher, without playing, but following the student's conducting, gives a reflection of the results of this conducting and explains how far the student's gestures are wrong, clumsy, or inappropriate. But soon, in proportion as the student acquires the needful mastery, inner (conceptive) and outer (technique of conducting), the master will actually present the music according to the way in which the student conducts. He will do it by singing or whistling; but always the intensity must be that indicated by the student. Then will the tiro first experience the correlation between productive motion and sounding music, and gradually learn to watch the actual effects of his gestures and compare these with the ideal conceptions which they ought to transmit.

The use of a pianoforte is intentionally excluded. The student's imagination must be given the widest scope. And through his being restricted to the bare rhythm and melody of the music, without the background provided by harmony, his capacity to conceive is strengthened.

To stimulate the conceptive activity, the student must be made to sing audibly what he is conducting. He must be compelled, every time he performs or repeats an exercise, to do so not only with equal, but if possible with increased intensity. When powerful, perfectly clear conception has become for the student a matter of course, he need no longer sing except inwardly; and he must be made to consider his gestures as the sole active means of utterance, until the moment when all his conceptions of tones automatically become motions, and even the slightest shades will begin to become perceptible in his conducting motions despite his adhering to plain basic metric gestures.

At first the student must conduct by heart. It does not at all matter how long or short a portion he has mastered. But he must have mastered this portion down to its utmost smallest ramifications, and hear it within himself as clearly in its harmony as in its rhythm and melody. The student's conducting clearly reveals the grade of his inner hearing: a misunderstood cadence, an undetected harmonic plan, cannot materialize into representative gestures; and then the watchful teacher will know at once, on the mere strength of the student's 'soundless' gestures, where the subject-matter of the work remains lifeless within the student.

To learn even a portion by heart requires practice, especially as it implies mastering the score down to the most minute details. The best way to set to work is to study the score a first time from the general musical point of view, taking into account the structural principles but not the orchestral setting. The next step is to consider the orchestral groups separately and study them thoroughly, one by one—strings, woodwind, brass, and percussion. The student must not miss one single accent, however slight, nor any one of the many hardly noticeable indications which, after the time of Bach, began to adorn orchestral parts. Having developed the habit of this patient detail work, he will soon acquire, besides a sure mastery of the score, the capacity quickly to perceive parallel relations. Thus his work will be thorough and carried out economically, and he will learn to acquire a remarkably faithful mastery of scores. At this point he may start attempting to embody his conceptions in actual conducting—which he can now do calmly and thoughtfully.

When learning to conduct by heart, the student must accustom himself from the outset to imagine the orchestra before him, to visualize its disposition, and to conduct accordingly. The first violins play on his left, the tone of the bassoons comes from the right and from the depths of the orchestra, the trumpets and trombones are in the farthest corner on the right, the 'celli and double-basses extend diagonally from the middle leftwards to the background. Naturally the above indications represent just an average case, one which commonly occurs nowadays. The only important things are that the student should feel and hear his orchestra in terms of space, that his movements should be related with the position of the players to whom they refer, and that his eyes should always have a firm hold of them.

A watchful eye establishes the strongest possible link between conductor and orchestra. The eye instantaneously strengthens the link with the players who have to stand out either because they have a solo to play or because they must play energetically. The eye, ever present, induces calmness and concentration, makes for sureness of entries, urges players to intensity. By learning to conduct by heart, the student will acquire the capacity to keep his eyes free for this purpose, and thence, the habit of controlling the orchestra with his eyes.

We come now to the practice of conducting as it can be described and taught by the method set forth in the foregoing chapters. Our examples are Beethoven's First Symphony, Strauss's 'Till Eulenspiegel', and Stravinsky's 'L'Histoire du Soldat', the pocket scores published by the Vienna 'Philharmonia' being used.

C. PRACTICAL EXAMPLES

1. BEETHOVEN: FIRST SYMPHONY, FIRST MOVEMENT

Adagio molto and *Allegro con brio.*

Task.

Learn the twelve-bar Introduction (*Adagio molto* ♪ = 88) by heart and present it by gestures. Firstly, the harmonic meaning of this bold beginning has to be comprehended. The harmonic scheme consists of progressions whose characteristic feature is the lack of harmonic definition. Cadences are started in a great variety of ways, and end deceptively. The very first chord, a chord of the tonic, has the minor seventh B flat affixed to it, and is thus turned into the dominant seventh of F major. Then, by way of a continuation apparently leading back to C major, comes the chord of the dominant, which however does not lead to C major but is followed by the deceptive cadence V–VI. And only then does a full close occur: on the sixth degree of C major, which becomes the second of G major, the broad V–I develops but only to carry us on to G major instead of finally stabilizing C major.

192

Bars 1–4.

The first thing is to learn to carry out the upbeat and downbeat as these have to be used in the first bar.

The student will begin with a precise quaver-upbeat. In order to accustom him forthwith to indicate the right tempo, he must be made to sing the first bar before starting his first motion, and so to obtain the upbeat, in a measure, from the very music. This upbeat must bring in a definite *f* entry of the whole orchestra. It must be given the form of a *staccato* beat; and it must occur again before the second bar.

The analysis of the harmonic structure of the Introduction has shown the transitional character of the cadential progressions. Thence, the closes marked can be but apparent closes, and must assume no character of finality.

In the first and second bar the fifth quaver (the second strongest part of the bar) must be taken unaccented, as a dying out. This is shown in the music itself by the fact that both cadential progressions begin, not with an upbeat (as they should according to their inner tendency), not on the third crotchet, but on 'one' and then, naturally, decrease.

Let us always remember that the natural starting-point of the motions is the norm which determines them. The firm downbeat 'one' corresponding to the *staccato* upbeat will be followed by the beating, with a minimum of motion, of the following quavers. These are not to be actually 'conducted'; time is beaten but nothing takes place. But the change in the harmony on 'five' must be marked in the conducting; the fourth quaver leads on upbeatwise, with a slight swerve, to the endbeat on 'five', thus:

Then the same course is repeated: 'six' and 'seven' are to be indicated with a minimum of motion (just counted), and 'eight' introduces, by means of a *staccato* upbeat, the following, similar bar.

With the third bar we learn a new kind of upbeat, and with the fourth a new endbeat. The *crescendo* entry of the wind in the third bar must

193

take place softly and sing: therefore the upbeat preparing it must have a *legato* character:

But the quavers that have to be counted in the course of this third bar play a part in its melodic and dynamic expansion, and develop slowly from small *legato* motions into *f* broadly beaten quavers.

On 'five' and 'seven' the melody moves towards the next bar; both times, intensifying upbeat motions prepare these advances, up to the climax which is reached on the downbeat of the fourth bar.

So far, we have been using the right hand only. Even thus, it was possible to deal with the *fp* in the first bar (the direct consequence of a *staccato* beat is that it shortens the vibrating tone; here it brings the vibrating *forte* down to *fp*). In order to exercise even more control over the orchestra, the left hand may be used in every one of the bars so far dealt with. At the moment of the first downbeat (that is, after the upbeat given by the right hand), let the student raise the left in a *staccato* motion a little beyond the normal starting-point of the beat, the palm of the hand turned outwards to moderate the orchestra. During the slight indications of count that follow, the left hand is allowed to sink back slowly; and on 'four', this hand takes up, jointly with the right, the sideways endbeat.

On 'six', 'seven', and 'eight' the left hand remains down, unconstrainedly. It deals with the second bar exactly as with the first. In the third bar it is used to intensify the singing tone, being left open and compelling, from the fifth quaver onwards; it marks, upwards and to the left, the melodic movement on 'five' and 'seven', and then the fist is closed to perform, together with the right hand, the endbeat on 'one' in the fourth bar. This way of using the left hand is purely expressive and representative: while the right counts out every quaver, the left merely gives a separate representment of the *crescendo* in the second half of the third bar and of its decisive development on the third and fourth crotchets.

This is really a representation of the music, but not one of an external kind: indeed, the action of the left hand must always take place as if the very power of the tone about to sound was directly becoming creative. The left hand must be used only when the student feels that he is holding within it the very tone that he wants to ring out. And it is only when the representative gesture is the complete fulfilment of an inner necessity that the orchestra directly comprehends it and feels its necessity.

We said that the fourth bar introduces to us a new kind of endbeat. In its beginning the following problem lies hidden: the chord struck by the whole orchestra ends with the second quaver, but the first violins continue, singing the third quaver of the melody (the G), and following up directly with the pattern in quavers which runs into the fifth bar. Therefore, two endbeats must follow upon one another, and despite the first the violins must continue, *f*. This can be brought about only if both arms are used in different ways. The left hand must perform the down-beat, and afterwards, still clenched, rise quickly and victoriously sustain the high G of the first violins. It is only after 'three' that it sinks again with a final endbeat, leaving the right hand to take charge alone of the sequel. Meanwhile the right, having counted out the first two quavers and marked a quick endbeat on the second, has remained inactive during the third quaver (the high G of the first violins) so as to con-centrate the whole attention upon the first violins. Then, it takes up the motion with the fourth quaver, and to the left. Thus we not only have represented exactly the two different endings (on 'two' and 'three') but have been able to transmute into suitable motions the distinction, in the fourth bar, between the struck chord and the melody upbeat.

Let us determine what these four bars have taught us:

(1) Both kinds of upbeat.
(2) Both kinds of endbeat.
(3) The use of the left hand.
(4) The independent use of both hands.
(5) The difference between representative (expressive) motions and motions that merely keep time.
(6) The increase of the amplitude of motion in the *crescendo*, and its decrease and wane at the end of cadences.

We have used the *staccato* form of the upbeat before the beginning of the first and second bars, the *legato* form before the beginning of the

195

third; the 'applied' expressive upbeat before 'five' and 'seven' on the third bar served the purpose of articulation, and after the *f* endbeats in the fourth bar the purpose of organizing into periods.

The *legato* endbeat serves (in 'applied' form) for the cadence endings in the first two bars; the *staccato* endbeat is used after 'two' and 'three' in the fourth bar. And despite the fact that all ending motions occur within the course of bars, every one of them calls for the use of the perfect pause-ending (no. 1, p. 170).

The left hand is used in the first bar as a moderator, to achieve the *f p*. In the *crescendo* in bar 3, and with the sustained note of the violins in bar 4, it is used for expressive, formative representation. The independence of both hands made it possible to give, in bar 4, two endbeats in immediate succession; and in the same bar, to differentiate the dynamic and the melodic functions respectively: the former is exemplified by the pause of the violins coming as the crowning of the first three bars, the latter when the fifth quaver leads on to the sequel.

An increase in the amplitude of the motion represented the *crescendo* in the third bar, and the decrease in amplitude and strength rendered the dying out of the cadences in the first and second bars possible.

Bars 5–7.

With the upbeat of the first and second violins to the fifth bar, there is a new development: the music proceeds in quavers (in the bass) over which the threefold melodic rise softly extends its canopies.

At first the left hand remains inactive, except perhaps to rise in a faint moderating gesture directed towards the oboe, the clarinet, or the horn, in case their tone should threaten to cover that of the flute and bassoon giving out motif-patterns. But the entry of these is regulated by the conductor's eye; and it is only with the fourth quaver of the seventh bar that his left hand rises again, moving higher and higher, marking a slow *crescendo*, to the big, singing upbeat motion on 'eight'.

From the fifth bar onwards, the right hand must carefully represent the melodic curves in the violins. Up to the semiquavers in the second halves of the bars, we have, in all three bars, simple melodic patterns encircling the rising notes: B (fifth bar), C (sixth), and D (seventh).

There must be no *crescendo* until the third quaver is reached, but a softly dying out singing tone. In other words, after the heavy downbeat the *legato* quavers 'two', 'three', and 'four' must come as mere aftermaths of this big motion, merely marking time. The fifth, however, will expand slightly, so as to give time for the first of the upbeat semiquavers to sound at leisure.

It is important to avoid wrong *crescendi* in the fifth and sixth bars; this is prevented by moderating upward motions of the left hand. When the melody rises in pitch, there always is a tendency to increase the volume. This tendency must steadily be opposed. Here it is particularly important to counteract it, because the intensity of the great song progression in the seventh bar, leading up to C major, should not be anticipated.

Moreover, the student should acquire from the start the habit of economy when dealing with *crescendi*, and never exaggerate them. When, as in this case, the objective is no more than a *forte*, care must be taken that motions and tone should increase barely perceptibly, so that the last step to the *forte* should really constitute an apex.

The points brought out by these three bars are:

(1) The inclusion of the eye's activity.
(2) The avoidance of wrong *crescendi*, and the keeping down of tones that might prove 'covering'.
(3) The intensive yielding of the motion to shades in the melody.
(4) Thrift in *crescendo*.
(5) Emphasis on decisive gestures.

In bar 5 three things are happening which must be watched simultaneously: the movement of the violins playing the melody with ornaments (interpreted and led by the right hand); the entry of the oboe, clarinet, and horn (indicated and regulated as to volume by the left); and the singing of the flute and bassoon, which is controlled by the eye. Naturally, the student's eye has been kept busy throughout the previous bars, regulating and marshalling; but now for the first time it fulfils an independent function, bringing out solo instruments.

The use of the left hand is extended in bars 5 and 6. The moderating gesture, already acquired with reference to fp, will be used soothingly,

197

in passing—as a preventative, lest the violins mark wrong *crescendi*, and as a corrective, in case the sustained notes of the wind, in bar 5, should rise so as to 'cover' up other parts.

The arabesques around the high B, C, and **D** at the beginning of bars 5, 6, and 7, is to be represented so that the quavers following the down-beat (that is, either the main note or its suspension) should be definitely expiratory—that is, be indicated by beats that decrease and merely mark time. Conversely, the singing upbeat semiquavers must be given by soft, expressive *legato* motions so that they come out calmly and consciously.

The economics of the *crescendo* and of the corresponding motions are particularly important, because orchestral players have a general tendency to make *crescendi* and *decrescendi* fitfully instead of con-tinuously; for instance, instead of distributing the increase regularly throughout a whole bar, they will carry it out prematurely, reaching the full volume of sound before reaching the actual climax, which then will be given, at best, a volume equal to that already reached. Conversely, *diminuendi* are nearly always carried out so as to give each note a lesser degree of loudness than is given to the foregoing, but a degree that remains the same throughout; the result is a decreasing series of grades, but not a continuous unbroken *decrescendo*.

The student must also notice that *decrescendi* are usually made to decrease too little and too slowly, exactly as *crescendi* are exaggerated and taken too quickly.

The decisive gestures that have to be emphasized are those that mark the culmination and the final point of developments. Therefore, here, the *f* reached after the rises in the third and seventh bars must both times be represented by a downbeat which surpasses the foregoing *crescendo* gestures not only in amplitude, but also in comprehensive energy.

Bars 8–12.

Until now, harmonic and melodic motions, cadence-forming groups, and flowing melody have been contrasted with one another. Henceforth, they are placed in closer relationship. In bars 8 and 10 the tendency towards cadences reasserts itself, evasively in bar 8 but strongly and leading to the goal in bar 10. The chords have acquired a melodic character and are closely bound to one another (as shown by the indication '*ten.*'). Conversely, the singing ninth bar has acquired increased harmonic significance and leads over the deceptive cadence on the sixth degree to a decisive final cadence. In the eleventh bar we encounter, through this cadence, the apex of the Introduction, whose intensity must surpass all previous *forte* effects.

In bar 12 the *p*, *unisono* design of the strings rising to the G, the fundamental note of the chord, must not have this G for its goal, but reach it from the first note of the design, the lower G, as if gradually dying out as it proceeds. The semiquavers must go *decrescendo* rather than expand; and exactly as the initial restlessness of the harmonic motion is smoothed out to the plain dominant tonic progression, so do these singing semiquavers roll back into themselves.

At bar 8 the right hand beats the chords with full, soft, cantabile quaver motions, preparing the entry of each new chord by an upbeat; the left, after the downbeat on 'one', promptly rises up again, and stays up to represent the four *tenuto* chords. When the first of these is quite near its end, the left hand, by a quick upbeat indication, gives the entry of the second; in this high position it must concentrate and encompass this second chord exactly as it had the first. It is only the fourth and last chord in the bar that must be given—at the very last moment, when it has run its course—a decisive upbeatlike endbeat. This ending must induce no break, but simply mark the duration of the *forte*; it must therefore occur after the right hand has beaten the eighth quaver, immediately before the *subito p* in the next bar.

Bars 9 and 10, intensified counterparts of bars 7 and 8, begin the *crescendo* on 'three'; the setting gives predominance to the woodwind and horns. In the stronger cadence in bars 10–11 the increased intensity expresses itself almost as a *crescendo*. The *crescendo* in bar 9 is represented by the left hand coming in on 'four' and beating together with the right, all four quavers in the second half of the bar. At the apex (bar 11) both hands perform an emphatic downbeat, after which the left quickly rises again, to fall back during the following *decrescendo*, so that the right alone beats the second half of the bar. At bar 12 the left hand is used to moderate, and stave off, a possible wrong *crescendo* in the strings.

At bar 11 the horn pattern is watched over by the conductor's eye. In these five bars the important points are:

(1) The determination of various degrees of *crescendo*.
(2) The determination of various degrees of intensity in harmony.
(3) The representation of the *decrescendo*.
(4) The immediate passage from *f* to *subito p*.

The same *crescendo* from *p* to *f* may vary in intensity according to the speed at which it takes place. In bars 3 and 7 it is spread over the whole bar; but at bar 9 it is given only one half of the bar. From the point of view of conducting, this reduction of the time allotted to the carrying out of a *crescendo* expresses itself through the representative motions increasing in amplitude and gaining intensity at double the pace.

At bar 8 the cadence begins with a full-weight tonic chord, whose *f* represents the climax of the previous *crescendo*. This chord is the very centre of gravity of the bar, which accordingly contains no possibility of further harmonic intensification. At bar 10 the corresponding cadential motion starts with the chord of the sixth degree, leading with a strong forward impulse to the second inversion in the next bar. This cadence has a distinct *crescendo* character, and its representation calls for strong impelling upbeat motions before every chord.

The *decrescendo* in bar 11 is expressed by the right hand's decreasing the amplitude of its gestures and by the left's quietly sinking until it becomes motionless on 'five'.

The passage from *f* to *p subito* (bar 8) is to be achieved as follows: the right hand beats the last quaver without rising as it normally should, but simply repeating, endbeatwise, the gesture performed on 'seven'; and meanwhile, the left performs, after 'eight', an upbeatlike endbeat (as for the third kind of pause endbeat). Thus the right, having stopped as explained, is ready to start, nearer to the body, the *p subito* quavers of the ninth bar.

In this first lesson we have tried to impart everything that can be learnt by tuition. The results are so considerable, that our previous assertion, 'twelve bars thoroughly studied and completely mastered from the technical point of view provide the principles for dealing with a whole range of every recurring problems', has gained fresh force.

Further work will confirm it over and again. The student, on the strength of what he has learned, is now capable of representing without assistance the greater part of the *Allegro con brio* and to find his own solutions of new problems.

Practice lesson.

The interpretation, in conducting by heart, of the first half of the *Allegro con brio* (pp. 3–13, to the repeat sign).

Pages 3–6.

The *Allegro con brio* ($\underset{\smile}{} = 112$) begins with the last four demisemi-quavers of the introduction. These can be taken in two ways: either as the proper conclusion to bar 12, to be used as motif in the sequel; or as the beginning of the *allegro*, the starting-point of the new tempo. The first conception is confirmed beyond a doubt by the fact that the theme never appears without this four-note upbeat; and against the second we have Beethoven's own metronomic indications, $\mathcal{J} = 88$ and $\mathcal{J} = 112$, which show that the minim must be taken almost half again as quick as previously the quaver. The solution is to consider the whole of bar 12 as an expiration, continuing the *decrescendo* of bar 11. The rise of the *unisono* strings to the G corresponds to the previous descent of the horns, *decrescendo*, from the same G and constitutes a continuation with further decrease. At the beginning of the twelfth bar the left hand takes charge of the strings' entry with a slight *legato* upbeat; without further motion, it keeps them down to *p* until it rises, with 'three' and 'four', slowly, in a moderating gesture, up to midheight, stopping exactly beneath the natural starting-point of the conducting motions. Meanwhile the right hand, by means of small *legato* strokes, has counted the metric units (the sonorous advance of the wind on 'five' being achieved by the eye), and performs 'seven' (as a quiet endbeat) to the left, towards the centre, so as to end the motion exactly at the starting-point of the motion for the last quaver—the upbeat of the *Alla breve*. The left hand indicates the ending on 'seven' by moving closer to the body, but remains motionless during the upbeat.

In this transition the art consists in combining endbeat and upbeat indications. The *Allegro con brio* is to be started quietly and restrainedly, the full speed being developed only when the *ff* on p. 4 is reached. In any case avoid starting the *Allegro* so hurriedly as to detract from the gathering-up effect of the entry of C major, *fortissimo*. For with this entry (p. 4, bar 7) all the forces of the *Allegro* must for the first time come into full action: the dynamic climax (*ff*), the consolidation of the main key (C major), and the steady measure of the tempo (the accompanying quavers of the strings).

The first four bars of the *Allegro* must be conducted by the right hand in precise, not too sharp, *staccato* minim beats. Meanwhile, the left must mark by downward motions, carried farther down every time, the entries of the chords. Having reached its lowest point, this hand, after the ending downbeat of the right, starts on 'two' of bar 5, upbeatwise and steadily rising, to conduct the *crescendo* of the wind, which it interrupts, in bar 6, by an upbeatlike endbeat, while the right begins with the second half of this sixth bar, to conduct the strings. Naturally, the eye must watch both groups—woodwind and strings—as they enter.

The same course is repeated from bar 7 to bar 12; but here the right hand conducts the whole of the *crescendo*—bar 12, during whose second half the left, with clenched fist, rises preparatory to a downbeat for the *sfz*, which ($\downarrow$.) it concludes on 'two' with an endbeat. At bar 13 the motions of the right, after a light *sfz* measure, forthwith resume their *p* character, while the left further emphasizes the *sfz* at bars 3 and 5 on p. 4, up to the moment when, in the *crescendo* bars preceding the *ff*, both hands together suddenly develop their full power.

All the *sfz* except the first arise out of an even *p*, without preliminary *crescendo*. Therefore no intensifying upbeats should precede them. In order nevertheless to mark them strongly each time, the left hand must rise each time on the upbeat from the waiting position, where it had previously rested, to the starting position, but rather closer to the body, and from there beat the *sforzandos* forwards and downwards.

Bar 6, p. 4, affords a typical Beethoven problem: the *crescendo* transition, in one bar only, from a long *p* to a no less prolonged *ff*. In order to achieve the intended thorough effect, everything must be kept back during the foregoing bars—motion, inner power, and intensity of tempo. And then all these elements must rise, in the shortest time, to their utmost degree, and, gathered up, reach with the cadence pulses in the next bar the apex of C major. The entry of this key is emphasized by an upbeat motion, whose amplitude and marshalling character must exceed all that had come before. This gesture is to be a maximum to which all foregoing gestures are to be subordinated.

But this grand C major suffers from the fact that in the sequel, the strings and woodwind, corresponding to one another, come out with unequal strengths; and the twofold entry of the brass and timpani might smother all the rest. Again we conduct strings and woodwind separately: the strings with the right hand, which carries on with the metre, the woodwind, as before, with the left. And as, especially, the *ff* quavers of the accompanying strings, in the bars in which the woodwind play, are too loud, the left hand should direct towards the violas, 'celli, and double-basses, immediately after the downbeat, the *fp* moderating sign already used in the Introduction. With bar 3, on p. 5, the left hand begins to take charge of the wind. The right, after having given the accent, conducts this bar to its end, and the following 'one' with a *fp* motion. After this, it turns, with a moderating gesture, upbeatwise, to the brass and timpani, before the beginning of bar 5. And at the end of this bar it again takes charge of the strings with a sharp *ff* upbeat.

The twenty bars we have just surveyed have raised hardly any new technical problems. The main points were:

(1) The entirely independent use of the two arms (for different groups and degrees of loudness);
(2) The various kinds of *sfz* (*p*, *crescendo*, *sfz*, and *p*, *subito sfz*);
(3) The exploding *crescendo* (transition from *p* to *ff*);
(4) Modifications carried out by conducting.

The independence of the two arms for characterization purposes is so important, that we have had to infringe the main principle of conducting, that 'the right hand has to mark all metric values'. In bar 5 of the *Allegro* (p. 5) the motions of the left coming in to conduct the *crescendo* of the woodwind are more expressive than purely metrical; but meanwhile the right hand remains quite motionless and starts, upbeatwise, only with the quiet time-keeping *staccato* beats concerning the strings. Naturally distributions such as this are possible only when they are useful and come naturally. When it has been possible to resort to them, the gathering-up resumption of the use of both arms becomes conducive to greater concentration and power.

Special interest attaches to bar 5 on p. 5, in which the independent action of the two hands represents three different activities of the three instrumental groups respectively. The left forcibly conducts the wood-wind; the right, preventatively, has moderated the entry of the brass and timpani, and immediately afterwards prepared, by a strong upbeat gesture, the *ff* melody of the violins that follows. It might be added that here the *p* and *ff* gesture for brass and strings should not follow one another without transition; on the contrary, the wind, after having been moderated, must be carried on, by energetic *crescendo* motion, to its goal, to 'one' of the next bar (the beginning of the repeat of the period).

The various kinds of *sfz* must be accurately differentiated. This applies not only to the two kinds considered above (*p crescendo sfz* and *p subito sf*), but to all degrees of strength in *sfz*. A *sfz* arising from a *p* will call for a different degree of strength than one arising on *mf*, *f*, *ff*, or *pp*. The exploding *crescendo* from *p* to *ff* is tremendous in its effect if despite its velocity it is kept continuous. This evenness of increase is hard to achieve; usually one hears, instead of it, either

$$\|p \underline{\hspace{0.5cm}} \boxed{f}\| ff \text{ or } \| p \boxed{ff} \| ff$$

Nothing is more relative than the sonority values of the various instruments and groups in the orchestra. If one is dull, if another gives out too much intensity of expression, the relationship between *p* and *f* is altered instantaneously; the distance from the one to the other is lengthened or shortened.

The ear of the conductor, as his chief means of gauging and watching over the music, can never be too alert, either to restrain or spur forward the progress (and thereby the tone) of the various instruments, as occasion arises. Therefore, let the student note that corrective adjustments during conducting are one of the conductor's most important tasks. These have to be carried out either by virtue of his previous experience of certain passages, or intuitively, on the strength of what is taking place at the very moment.

Pages 6–9.

The *crescendo* on p. 6 must be conducted with prudence. As we had already reached a *ff*, the *crescendo* must consist of an increase in intensity rather than in sonority. This is shown in the music by the impatient rush upwards from note to note up to the high C (after the second quaver in the third *crescendo* bar). Technically, this increase in intensity is achieved by marking small, eager subdivisions of the minims in the last *crescendo* bar—not rigorous indications of metre but rather expressive interpretation. And the *crescendo* must start gradually, and not prematurely, so as to gather intensity as it nears its goal.

There is nothing new to be said about bars 2 to 5, p. 7. But it should be noticed that the following end-bar (bar 6) gathers up the orchestral groups into a climax and therefore calls for the co-operation of both arms. The motions should not be too short and *staccato* but rather insistent and *portato*-like, corresponding to the amplitude and movement of the quavers in the bass. It is only the beats of the second and third bars on p. 8 that have to be short and final.

In the third bar the second subject begins. The upbeat for it must be given a duration slightly longer than that of the preceding downbeat, so as to produce a barely perceptible break—the motion, after the downbeat, must pause, and then the right hand alone continues in broad *portato* beats. The *sfz* in bars 8 to 11 (again occurring amidst the general *p*) are marked by the left hand and the right alternately. The left, which had remained motionless, marks the *sfz* of the wind on 'two', downwards, starting half-way below the normal starting-point and moving slightly towards the body. Correspondingly, the right marks light accents on the second half of each bar by impelling, upwards motions. The *sfz* of the bass in the last bar is again marked by the left hand.

Before the four *f* bars on p. 9, the left hand rises, upbeatwise, to take its part in beating the three *f* minims and accent them, while the right, by an impelling motion, brings out and emphasizes the following quavers —making the downbeat in bar 6 very short and final, as if the second crotchet-value in the bar bore not a crotchet, but a semiquaver followed by a dotted quaver rest.

The *sfz* on p. 9 (after a repetition of the bars just dealt with) and the immediately following *crescendo*, which rises to *ff*, call for notice. The *crescendo* so strongly brought out by repeated upbeat attacks that its quavers must carry out the final cadence with great force. To this effect, expressive subdivision of the end-motion should once again be resorted to.

We have now learned:

(1) The intensity *crescendo* (achieved by means of expressing, representative, subdividing motions);

(2) The intensity ending (achieved by the same means);

(3) The *portato* beat;

(4) The articulating upbeat-accent;

(5) The articulating endbeat;

(6) The representation of *sforzandi* occurring in immediate succession (achieved by the use of the two hands).

Intensifications starting on a *ff* may be achieved either by actual *crescendo*, or in conclusions, by a heightening of tone-expressiveness, induced by expressive representation. Subdivision of the normal beats is the natural way of inducing this ever-increasing rise which takes in every element in the music.

Half-way between the extremes represented by *staccato* beat and *legato* beat there is the *portato* beat, as a link between them. According to the character of the music conducted, it may incline towards the form of the *staccato* motion or that of the *legato* stroke. Its variants are countless, as are the degrees between *legato* and *staccato*.

Upbeat and endbeat motions may serve the purposes of articulation. The upbeat, by an energetic impulse, may bring out the beginning of a segment; the endbeat, by the slightest possible extension, can bring out the expiration of a segment.

Syncopated accents, accents that do not coincide with the metre-beat, are represented by the left hand (which must be kept still before and after so doing); non-syncopated accents—those that coincide with the beat—by impelling motions of the right hand which indicates them.

Pages 9–13.

Exactly as the *f* pulses on p. 9 hark back to the first subject, so does the *pp* on p. 9 correspond to the calmer character of the second. Hence, the representing motions of the right hand are to be gentle and *portato*-like after the forcible ending on 'one', this latter having been carried out by the left hand with a sweeping downward motion which was immediately curtailed. The entry, on p. 10, of the oboe and bassoon, is to be indicated by the eye only, while the right hand continues its quiet *portato* motions. The left must not be used for these entries of the wind; if the *crescendi* of oboe or bassoon are too loud, it will be enough to bring the right hand closer to the body in a hushing motion, while beating; for the left must be kept ready to prevent the *crescendo* that usually starts with the third bar of the bass melody, as this melody rises in pitch.

It has already been said that players tend to identify upward motion with *crescendo*. Here it is particularly important absolutely to avoid an increase in volume, in order not to detract from the possibilities of intensification lying in the final three crescendo bars on p. 10. In order to give these three bars their full expansion, use the left hand from the start to intensify, expressively, the melody in the bass. The *f* conclusion must be emphasized, as an apex, by a decisively rising upbeat, to which the right, after the downbeat, responds with an impelling motion on 'two'. The accents in the first and second bar of p. 11 are to be indicated by sharp beats, after which the left marks the first beats of the bars, until both arms together rise to achieve a decisive downbeat for the *ff* (on p. 11). The following chords of the diminished seventh (bars 6 and 8, p. 11), whose harmonic intensity has a heightening effect, must both be 'attacked', to a certain extent, by a light accent-beat. The *unisono sfz* are to be taken with endbeats, as plain endings on the 'strong' part of the bar. But with the last of these, the motion rises upbeatwise, in order to prepare a full conclusion (p. 12, bar 3).

The following *p* bars are to be conducted by the right hand only, which for each *sfz subito* adds to the corresponding second minim-beats short sharp impelling motions. It is only with the last upbeat-crotchet, marked *ff* (p. 13), that the left rises, to mark it and to take part in the beating of the ending on 'one', after which it straightway reverts to the starting-point of the beats. From this moment the left conducts alone the *diminuendo* wind by downward motions for the minims. The right, which meanwhile has remained down, rises only to indicate the interrupting *ff* pulse of the strings, independently of the left hand, which is waiting a further *diminuendo*.

There remains to notice, with regard to the above points:

(1) The technical representation of melodic and harmonic changes;
(2) The use of identical downbeat-like motions for a continuous sequence of non-differentiated *sfz* values;
(3) The exchange of functions between the two hands.

Downbeat, upbeat, and accent are the elementary resources for the technical presentation of melodic and harmonic changes. The first four bars on p. 11 call for their alternate use, and so do the following six bars.

Sforzando notes that are equal in dynamic value and duration, such as occur in the first two bars on p. 12, are to be taken with downbeats only, each of which is forthwith followed by a return to the starting-point exactly as in the case of whole-bar beats.

The exchange of functions between the two hands is resorted to whenever two different, important relationships have to be represented simultaneously. In the present case, the two relationships are, for the left hand, the continuous *decrescendo* of the woodwind (p. 13), leading up to the repetition, and for the right hand, kept motionless, the waiting (characterized by the *ff* pulse) for this repetition.

Task.

Learn by heart and conduct the second half of the *Allegro con brio*.

Pages 13–18: working-out section.

The threefold repetition of the four-bar period which opens the working-out section is to be conducted by the right hand. It is advisable to add to each *f* downbeat, on the second part of the bar, an upbeat-like endbeat of the left hand. During this, the right hand rises almost imperceptibly to the starting-point of the beats, and thence represents, with a minimum of motion, the next three bars: the first *p*, merely marking the time, the second and third in light elastic beats setting forth the descending notes of the bars and the syncopation.

The two *fp* and *staccato* four-bar periods (p. 14, bar 12) are to be conducted by the right hand only with small, time-marking motions after the accented *fp* downbeat. Meanwhile, the left hand remains ready eventually to come in as a moderator; this especially applies to the fourth, concluding bars of both periods.

With the *pp* bars (p. 15) the left associates with the right, which, emphasizing the *pp*, has performed the upbeat heralding these bars with a preventative motion, directed towards the body.

At the seventh bar the left hand joins in the motion in big *crescendo* gestures, so as to help in really passing from *pp* to *ff* within the narrow space of two bars. It ends the *ff* with an upbeat-like endbeat, quickly turning into a *fp* indication. After this, the right alone beats time for the four *p* bars, while the eye supports and guides the first and second violins alternately. At the *f* on p. 16 the motions should be most carefully increased in compass and force, so as to preserve the difference between this *f* and the previous *ff* indicated by the two hands jointly. We determine the *sfz* of the first violins on p. 16, bar 3, by the impelling upbeat motion of the right hand already known to us; and with the *decrescendo* in bar 4, we turn the beats, by swiftly decreasing their amplitude, into light time-marking motions. These start the new, *p*, four-bar period, which is given out three times, and consists of two running *staccato* bars and two gliding *legato* bars. It is advisable, at the end of the four bars, to retard the movement slightly, so as to make possible a really fresh start with a downbeat for the next period. This, however, does not apply to the end of the third period, which passes without transition into three single bars (*portato* beats) and in the fourth rises, with the help of the left hand, to a speedily reached *fortissimo*. To this *crescendo* (p. 17) applies what has been said before of the intensity *crescendo*; the entry of the *ff* must likewise be conducted with a big downbeat.

Again we have strings and woodwind in opposition, the one group attacking *staccato* and the other singing *legato*, and again the hands represent these contrasts separately, while the eye keeps the brass under control. In order to impart greater impetus to the upward storming *staccato* quavers on p. 17, bar 8, take the second minim endbeatwise, with a half-length motion to the left, sideways, and downwards; then, on the fourth crotchet, raise the hand in an energetic upbeat. The *legato* beats of the left should not be too ample, but simply tense and forceful; for the tone of the thinner woodwind must not be dropped prematurely, but on the contrary be sustained to the very end in a concentrated *ff* cantabile. With the entry of the semiquavers in the strings, the right hand starts conducting again (on the second half of this bar).

In the second and third bars on p. 18 the left hand gives the important *ff sfz* as follows: the actual downbeats are barely indicated, and it is only for the second *sfz* crotchet, i.e. on the 'weak' part of the bar, that the left hand is driven sharply down, forthwith to rise again, upbeatwise, for the second minim.

The right hand joins in for the gathering-up *ff* pulses. After the last of these it merely beats time, in slight, decreasing motions, until the end of the *decrescendo* in the woodwind. During this *decrescendo* the motion of the left hand has changed to moderating pure and simple. This hand has remained raised after the downbeat of bar 6, but on the second half of bar 7 resumes conducting, with an upbeat, to lead the woodwind to the repeat, strongly intensifying them. With the upbeat for the strings, the right hand joins in, and thenceforth again takes charge, in the normal fashion, of the metre indications.

The particular points to be observed in this working-out section are:

(1) The dynamically formative upbeat;
(2) The endbeat providing motif-articulation;
(3) The grouping of periods;
(4) The subdivision of beats for expressively representative purposes.

We shall often resort to the upbeat that dynamically indicates the *pp*, as we have found it, p. 15, before the fifth bar. Rationally used, its effect is certain if it is performed by motion direct towards the body and not, upbeatwise, high up into the air.

The endbeat for purposes of motif-articulation, as for the first *f* chord at the very beginning of the working-out is another indispensable resource for detaching from one another dynamic or melody-building elements that are associated, but contrasting, in the same period. Notice its performance by the left hand.

The technique for grouping into consecutive order periods that begin with fresh starts is of general importance. The process employed to that effect (a sudden retardation of the motion on the upbeat, so as to ensure a really 'beginning' downbeat) shows the wealth of shades that can be represented by means of the few fundamental motions in use.

The subdivision of beats as means of expressive representation occurs on p. 17, bar 8, and p. 18, bars 2 and 3. In the first instance it is carried out by the right hand, and serves to impart increased impetus to the rush of the strings in quavers. In the second case the left hand uses it to represent the syncopated *ff sfz* of the singing woodwind.

Pages 18–27: Recapitulation and Coda.

All that was said before applies to the recapitulation *ff*, except that the upbeats for the first and second bars must be performed in subdividing, reinforcing motions. At bar 5, p. 19, in order to achieve a precise, effortless *p* entry of the strings, use the method of arresting motion after the drive of the beat, already mentioned several times, and not an accenting motion, however slight. Again the orchestral groups are to be represented separately by the two hands. The above-mentioned entry of the strings is marked by one single gesture of the right hand, which afterwards remains motionless up to bar 8 on p. 19, when it again takes sole charge of the conducting and beats the following bars *crescendo*, alone. With the *ff* of the woodwind (p. 19, last bar but one), the left comes in for the last three *ff* minims, and afterwards does nothing except join in marking the downbeats in bars 1 and 3, p. 20, and the *sfz* in bars 5 and 6. The *ff sfz* in bars 1 and 3 are marked by the right hand in slight subdividing sideways motions.

The second subject, which comes in p. 20, had been, in the exposition, prepared by a slight check on the downbeat preceding the upbeat for it. The preparation, on that occasion hardly perceptible, is now effected by the smallest possible introductory *decrescendo* of a quietening effect in the *unisono* strings, p. 20, bar 8. Notice that bars 5 and 6, p. 20, are to be conducted in sharp *staccato* beats, and the following two in broad, sustaining *legato* motions.

From the first four bars of p. 25 onwards, again use the left hand for the woodwind and *legato*, the right beating time for the strings and *staccato*. It is advisable, every time the right hand starts the motion by which it leads the strings, that the left should stop with a moderating gesture, and only start working again, upbeatwise, with the

211

woodwind on 'two' (p. 25, bar 5), in accordance with the articulation of the music.

Both hands, however, conduct the three *crescendo* bars, increasing both the loudness and the intensity, in order to lead with real grandeur into the forcible motions for the three two-bar attempts at cadences (p. 26) before the coda. These beats must not be too brief, but be *staccato pesante* gestures; otherwise the basses and 'celli will not come in ponderously enough. One must remember to bring the third cadence (p. 26, bars 5 and 6) to its end with a gathering up and increased strength.

The coda itself should be started with a big downbeat. In its first two bars, the right hand, working energetically and giving only sketchy indications of the subdivisional values, should induce the first violins, 'celli, and basses to give out the first part of the subject powerfully. In the third bar the eye should encompass and muster the brass and timpani; and in the fourth, the left hand, by an intensifying upbeat, should induce the woodwind to a corresponding *ff* and at the same time prepare the *sfz* entry of the second four-bar period. All this takes place three times. But it is only at p. 27, bar 6, that the crowning apex, *ff*, of the whole movement is reached. And there, for the first time, the amplest, most significant gesture that the conductor can achieve is to be used, having been deliberately kept in reserve and not even anticipated by any form of allusion. To reinforce it, the upbeat preceding its downbeat may be arrested a moment just after its start, so that the carrying out of 'one' may acquire a really decisive significance. The entry of the timpani on the second crotchet is to be indicated separately, by an inserted, accenting, small subdividing motion sideways. The semiquavers of the timpani must be given out distinctly as such and not degenerate into a quick *tremolo*.

All the chords in the last six bars are to be made conclusive. The rests after the chords (in the sixth, fifth, and fourth bars before the end) are no longer to be indicated by sharp upbeats—on the contrary, the conductor should practically restrict himself to giving the gathering-up downbeats. The last three chords are to be taken in even downbeats.

The analysis of the recapitulation and coda has shown:

(1) The increasing significance of subdivisions in beating;

(2) The increasing significance of a slight wait on the upbeat;

(3) The *staccato-pesante* beat for *ff* notes coming as afterbeats;

(4) The significance of the apex-marking gesture.

The indication of beat-subdivisions is continuously acquiring new force for expressive representation. With the entry of the Coda (p. 26, bar 7) it is used to impart additional energy to very small values; and at the apex it is used to impart crowning definition to the entry of the timpani.

Likewise, the slight wait after the start of an upbeat (or of a downbeat too) is acquiring greater significance. We used it, p. 27, to underline furthermore the apex-marking gesture.

By way of a new shade in *staccato* beats, we have the *staccato pesante*, to bring out important *ff* notes coming as afterbeats. It can be intensified by subdivisional beats. The apex-marking gesture must occur once only; both as imagery and as expression of power it must come as something quite fresh, and tower above all that came before.

The results of the above tuition and work are so rich in educational value for the student, that we may now consider him capable of solving problems for himself. Therefore, from now on, we shall refer only to any really new technical point in our survey of the remaining movements of Beethoven's First Symphony.

BEETHOVEN: FIRST SYMPHONY, SECOND MOVEMENT

Andante cantabile con moto (♪ = 120).

(*Score*, pp. 28–40.)

The distinctive character of the opening theme is a graceful *cantabile*. This, in performance, will tone down the contrast indicated by Beethoven himself, between *staccato* and *legato* within this theme, to approximately soft *portato* on the one hand and light *legato* without *crescendo* on the other. Yet, in conducting, the inner articulation of this melody has to be technically represented down to the smallest details. We start with a light, upbeat-like time-indicating preliminary motion on 'two', followed with a bigger movement for the actual beginning on 'three'. The definitely upbeat-like motif ♪ | ♩♪, whose musical centre of gravity rests, in the first two bars, on the *legato* upbeat quaver, calls for a downbeat on 'one' that will be merely indicative. After this the movement should immediately stop, so as to shorten the end quaver tied to the

213

upbeat quaver. The second quaver in each bar is to be beaten as an expiration, and is immediately followed by a fresh beginning on the upbeat quaver of the motif.

The third bar is to be represented, on 'one' and 'two', by the blunt *staccato* beats already used before; the fifth bar, without transition, by small stroking *legato* motions. Meanwhile, the left hand must be held in readiness to come in preventatively; for the tendency nearly always asserts itself to take the rising, singing *legato* in a *crescendo*.

The *sfz* on p. 29 are to be clearly marked by impelling motions of the right hand. The left is to join in only on the last bar but one for the *sfz* on 'three' (oboes), and also in marking the endbeats in the first and second bars of p. 30. For these two bars it is advisable to start all the three beats (on 'two', 'three', and 'one') slightly downwards although adhering to the normal direction:

In the *crescendo subito p* of the violins on p. 30 the right hand alone carries out the *crescendo*, the left joining in only on the last quaver before the *p*, with a quiet upward motion. Immediately before the beginning of the *p* bar, this motion, in the same high position, turns into a moderating *fp* gesture and then is carried slowly downwards. For the first four bars on p. 31 the right hand must give blunt *staccato* beats, coming to rest immediately and suggestive of shortening. Be very careful to avoid that favourite trick of the players of turning the rhythm

To this effect the blunt *staccato* motions prove helpful. By holding back every time and thus indicating directly, without transition, the following units, they reduce to a minimum the danger that the demisemiquavers of the upbeat, coming in too soon, should become triplet-semiquavers.

The entry of the timpani and trumpets on p. 31 is given by the eye. The end of the first part (the last two bars before the double bar) is to be conducted as an expiration, in slackening, dying-away endbeats.

With the beginning of the second part the left hand joins in, to moderate, while the beating is being performed downwards and close to the body. The right alone takes charge of the *crescendo*, and it is only the *ff* upbeat (p. 32, last bar) that is marked by both hands together. After the downbeat that follows, the left hand rises back quickly, to go down again, by decreasing degrees (*ff, f, mf*), to the *p* on 'one'. All the *subito sfz* are marked by impulses of the right hand, without preparatory upbeats, while the left hand restrains the strings from being influenced by the wind into carrying on the *sforzando* in bars 4, 6, and 8 of p. 33. Care should be taken to keep the whole passage down to *p*, the *sfz* coming in as mere accentuations. The upbeat-patterns ‖ ♪ ♫ ♪ ♫ ‖ in the last two bars of p. 33 must be accurately indicated and kept separate, as a *p* form of the motif without *crescendo*, and a *f* form of it without *diminuendo* respectively. The last quaver in each of them is to be taken in a holding-back, blunt *staccato* beat. This applies with even greater force to the diatonically descending alternations of strings and woodwind (p. 34, from bar 3)—in which, moreover, the left must carefully keep the flute down lest it should cover the oboes.

The left joins in again, upbeatwise, with bar 11, p. 34. It is kept high up to sustain and intensify this *f* bar, and goes down on 'one' in bar 12, taking this *f* in an endbeat. The same course is repeated in the following bars. Remember, from p. 35 onwards, to prepare the *pp* re-entry of the theme *pp* (leading the woodwind, here as in all similar cases, with the eye only). Here slight transitional moderating gestures of the left hand will help. The entry of the bassoon ‖*p* ＜ ＞‖ is given by the eye only while the left hand waits, ready to come in for the purpose of shading. The *crescendo* of the strings (bar 7) must be carried out very cautiously and only up to *p*), and is to be expressed mainly by a change from dance-like *staccato* to song *legato*. With the *pp* in bar 10, the motion of the right hand comes nearer to the body and is restricted in order to bring down the instruments' tone; and the left hand on this *pp* upbeat performs its moderating gesture downwards.

It is advisable to use the left hand for the *f* pulses of the timpani on the apex-like first bar of p. 40, but only after the *sfz*. In bars 2 and 3 the *f subito p* is achieved by means of an upbeat-like moderating gesture of the left hand (exactly as the *subito p*, p. 39, bar 8).

While the melody ends, *p*, the right hand marks time in lingering blunt *staccato* beats, and the eye leads the oboe. With the entry of the first violins the left hand comes in, upbeatwise, passes on forthwith, on 'one', to a moderating gesture, and represents the inner *decrescendo* of the descending first violins by slowly sinking, marking the time meanwhile.

Before the *pp* quavers of the first violins (sixth bar before the end) the left hand again performs a moderating gesture, slighter this time, by way of lingering conclusion of 'one'. After this, it is better to use the left hand and the right separately, for wind and strings respectively, and always with the lingering conclusive motions of the left on 'one'. The *subito f* at the end is conducted with a powerful impelling motion and a thorough endbeat, marking a break. The last *p* crotchet is to be quietly sustained, and after this comes an endbeat.

The new technical points we have discovered are:

(1) The way to represent a melody with shadings down to the smallest details (the theme on p. 28).

(2) The representative use of the endbeat (used in bar 1, p. 30, for every unit in the bar).

(3) The *crescendo subito p* (p. 30, last bar but one).

(4) The significance of the lingering, blunt *staccato* beat (to prevent ‖ ♩. ♫ ‖ being carelessly turned into ‖ ♪₃ ♪ ‖).

(5) The means of representing two-quaver melodic groups within the 3/8 bar (p. 34, bars 3 sq.).

(6) The means of representing *f subito p* by using the two hands differently:

    (*a*) within the course of a melodic progression (p. 34, last four bars);

    (*b*) when *f* and *p* are contrasted, to mark articulation and breaks (p. 40, bars 2–3).

(7) Motif articulation and dynamic articulation by means of both hands (*p* and *subito pp* sixth bar before the end; *subito f* and *subito p* in third and second bar before the end; and, in the same, 3/8 motif-shaping and 2/8 *f* end-shaping).

(8) Ending the beating of the final note with a definite endbeat, without conducting this note to its very end.

216

BEETHOVEN: FIRST SYMPHONY, THIRD MOVEMENT

Menuetto, Allegro molto e vivace ($\downarrow$ = 108).

(*Score*, pp. 41–7.)

Despite the title 'Menuetto', this movement is a real Beethoven Scherzo, in whole-bar time-units, as prepared by that wonderful expression of power and character, the Minuet in Mozart's G minor Symphony. In order to perform the whole-bar upbeat unequivocally and to set the tempo compellingly, the student should be made first to sing several bars of the beginning within himself, and then, without interruption, to start conducting. The left hand comes in at the bar in which the woodwind enter, so as to ensure a clear representation of the last two bars by means of one whole-bar upbeat and endbeat motion.

The same course is repeated in bars 3–4 and 7–8 of the second part. The right hand alone conducts bar 9, and for the *ff* both hands are used, leading up to the sharp endbeats. After this the right hand conducts alone, while the eye governs the *p* entries of the flutes.

From the *pp* onwards (p. 42, bar 14) the left hand performs with every beat (even those carried out by the right) a moderating gesture close to the body. The consecutive *pp* entries of bass and woodwind are marked by the eye. With the *crescendo* of the third entry of the bass, the right hand takes charge of this group and starts the *f* bar with an upbeat. Before the *ff* the left hand rises, sustaining this by remaining raised to the end, afterwards marking every *sfz* with a distinct downbeat. The sixth bar on p. 44 is conducted by the left hand in a conclusive manner with a sharp moderating upbeat-gesture. In order to carry out the following syncopations flowingly, the conducting should be in *portato* beats, which at the following *crescendo* change to sharp *staccato* beats. Bar 15 on p. 44 must be taken with an emphasizing downbeat. The fourth bar before the end of this page calls for an even more emphatic one, in which both hands join. The last two, actually concluding, bars are beaten, after a preparatory upbeat, with an apex-marking gesture downwards to mark the conclusion; and the beat for the last note must mark thorough finality.

In this transition to the Trio the beat dwells a brief while on the

217

concluding 'one', and then rises—very accurately in the new tempo—upbeatwise, in a precise *p portato* motion.

The *p sfz* on p. 45 is to be marked by an impelling motion of the left hand; and in the next bar this motion is continued in a gliding end-gesture, which ends close to the body. In this first part of the Trio, an accurate representation of the structure must be made in three eight-bar periods with various subdivisions (4+4 bars for the first and second periods respectively, 2+2+4 for the third). It is advisable to conduct the four initial bars in the first and second periods thus: for the first three, the right hand rises lightly, and forwards; it indicates the fourth upbeatwise, leads up to the fifth, the conclusion, and then stops while the left represents the bars given out by the strings (starting with 'two'), after the fashion of a *diminuendo* 4/4 consisting of whole-bar beats. The use of the right hand for the wind, and of the left for the strings, is continued through p. 46. In the fourth bar before the end of this page, a *ff* downbeat is to be used, and the left hand must mark additional emphasis for the *sfz*. Again the last two bars are to be taken in endbeats, and so that the last note should come as the conclusion of the foregoing *sfz* downbeat. Before the *Da Capo*, the hand waits and then brings in the repetition of the Minuet with a clear, upward whole-bar motion.

The new points are:

(1) The use of the whole-bar beat as an articulating upbeat or endbeat (p. 41, *f* bars of subject).

(2) Marking a *ff sfz* by means of the left hand (p. 43).

(3) Economy of intensification by means of variants in the motions (see p. 44, bars 7 sq.: *p portato* and *staccato* beats gradually gaining in sharpness; *f* downbeats, and co-operation of the left hand for the apex).

(4) Articulation of sections whose respective speeds are different, by means of lingering end-motions followed by distinct upbeats (Menuetto-Trio).

(5) Representation of period structure (first part of Trio).

BEETHOVEN: FIRST SYMPHONY, FINALE

Adagio (♩. = 63) *and Allegro molto e vivace* (♩ = 88).

(*Score*, pp. 48–64.)

The *ff* with pause that opens the *Adagio* is to be represented as forcibly as can be by the left hand, clenched and held high, without ever drooping or slackening the intensity concentrated in its action. Then, to end the pause, this hand goes down, and near to the body, in a broad, semi-concluding gesture. Then, after the pause-break, the right hand alone starts the *p* tentative upbeats. In order to avoid a change of ‖ ♫♩. ‖ into ‖ ♪₃ ♪ ‖ (and because a *staccato* is prescribed) again lingering, dull *staccato* beats are used here. They assume a *portato* character as the *crescendo* grows; and on the last semiquaver the left hand rises upbeat-wise and with a moderating *fp* gesture (p. 48, bar 4), while the right, with the *p subito pp* that follows, subsides in a diminishing motion. The pause on F of the first violins is to be ended with a slight but definite slide sideways, followed without transition, after the rest, by the upbeat motion on ‘two’, which starts the *Allegro*.

On p. 50, the brass and timpani, despite the foregoing *ff*, must play *f* and not louder. In order to keep them down and preclude unsuitable prominence, the right hand must conduct in light, elastic motions. The *sforzandi* on ‘two’ (to be marked by impelling motions) are important; as are the continuation bars at the end of p. 50, which come as interruptions, and whose ‘one’ is to be accented by lingering, sharp, downbeats.

When the *decrescendo* begins (p. 51), the left hand joins in on ‘one’ to sink back, close to the body, in an endbeat motion.

The four crescendo bars with the rising diatonic progression on p. 52 must be given great intensity and be magnified by the conductor's motions. After the accenting *sfz*, the left hand joins in, gathering up, for the entry on ‘two’ of the *ff*, and ends every crotchet in bars 11 and 12 on p. 52 with downward endbeats.

Care should be taken that in the following two four-bar segments (p. 52) the timpani and brass should not stand out too much. As before, lighter motions should be resorted to; but for bar 16, and bar 1 on p. 53, both hands should be used, so as to bring out these bars with endbeats. From bar 2 onwards, conduct the second violins with energetic impelling motions on 'two', and small but energizing subdivisional indications for every reappearance of the head of the subject winding its way upwards diatonically. The left hand is kept in reserve until it has to take charge of the *fp* on p. 53, which it does with a moderating end-marking gesture.

After the repetition, the motion in bars 4, 8, and 10, p. 54, lingers awhile after the downbeats and then proceeds farther with a distinct upbeat but without accenting. Before bar 10 (the *pp*) the left hand performs a moderating upbeat, brought close to the body. In the *ff* that follows, each melodic advance must be clearly represented by impelling motions —especially so the beginning of the repetition on 'two', fifth bar before the end of the page.

On p. 56, the *f*, bar 5, must be accurately differentiated from the *ff*, bar 9. The *sfz* are taken in big downbeats, the scales of the violins in impelling upward motions for their beginnings on 'two'. At the apex of this progression, the *pesante legato* (p. 57, bar 6) and the *staccato* quavers of the woodwind that immediately follow it (bar 10) must be clearly represented—the latter usher in, after an upbeat *fp* gesture of the left hand, the repetition, *p*.

The *ff* entry of the whole orchestra (p. 61, bar 1), which opens the culmination, must be brought out by a big, gathering-up downbeat. This is the point at which to prepare (this time by a continuous increase of both volume and intensity) and to use the one apex-gesture applying to both the crowning pauses. This gesture will be reinforced by the left hand being prudently kept in reserve until these very pauses, which it will come to mark with all its power.

On p. 61, antepenultimate bar, at 'two', the left hand performs a motion towards the body, to bring the tone down to *pp*, and in the last bar carries it back to *p*.

On p. 63, bars 6–9 must be performed *f*, not *ff*. Therefore, they are to be conducted with light, elastic motions, corresponding to the increasing sway of the coda as it rushes to its end.

After the *ff*, p. 64, bar 6, we have two intensifying *sfz* and the actual *ff* culmination of the end. This intensification can be achieved only if

220

a special gesture has been kept in reserve to summon once again—and this time more intensively—a full outburst of power.

This Finale has taught us nothing actually new: the student has learned so much through dealing with the previous three movements that he is able to achieve on his own, without further suggestions from the teacher, an adequate presentation of the fourth.

Before passing on to 'Till Eulenspiegel' we shall call attention to three vital points:

(1) The tempo must be not only correctly indicated, but correctly maintained. The student, therefore, must be made to represent quite strictly the selected tempo, remaining quite unaffected by anything that might influence him to the contrary. Only changes that are necessary and come quite naturally should justify a quickening or slowing of the speed. And it is only after he has learned to keep steadily to a basic tempo that he will be able naturally and easily to resort to changes of speed that seem to belong to the very nature of the works.

(2) In the course of our progress we have often run counter to our original principle that the right hand alone has to indicate the metre. This principle was set down in order to accustom the student always to represent metric patterns quite clearly and simply. Practice, however, soon made it necessary to differentiate instrumental groups, dynamic contrasts, technical processes of performance, &c., by means of supplementary motions of both arms working separately and differently.

(3) We shall no longer insist unconditionally that the student should thoroughly know by heart the scores he deals with. But he must have studied them thoroughly enough to have reached a stage at which a very little more work would enable him to conduct by heart. The score on his desk must serve as a hardly needful aid to memory; if used thus (which the student must now learn to do), a high degree of economy of labour will soon be achieved.

2. RICHARD STRAUSS: 'TILL EULENSPIEGEL'.

The problems raised by 'Till Eulenspiegel' from the conductor's point of view will be dealt with quite differently, in point of method, from those raised by Beethoven's First Symphony. We shall discuss nothing but matters not yet encountered; and in so doing we shall not follow the order in which they occur in Strauss's work, but arrange them in a special order, with references to the pocket-score in the same Philharmonia edition.

The technical resources available for the purpose of unequivocably representing the phrasing of any music are: the upbeat and endbeat, the *crescendo* and *diminuendo*, the impelling motion, and the lingering motion. These we use mostly in combination, e.g. for the two inserted motifs (of one bar and a half each) in the first three bars of p. 17, we use, by way of start, an impelling motion, which is, the first time, a quiet articulating downbeat (sinking lower than the downbeat on 'one' in the previous bar), but the second time an upbeat, aiming at bringing out, and quietly rising higher than the previous upbeats had risen. Both motifs end in expirations which are controlled by reducing *decrescendo* gestures.

The above example shows a complicated form of the simple case occurring in the first four bars of p. 15, where the two-bar phrases must be given their distinct beginnings and endings.

For the motif in bars 8–11, p. 59, use a combination of indicated *crescendo* gesture (to express motion towards the goal) and—at the end—almost lingering endbeat (after which the rest values are not to be conducted, but simply marked).

Use the *crescendo* motion deliberately for the entries of the wind, violas, and 'celli leading up to the culmination, with and after the last two and a half bars, pp. 74–5. Be thrifty at first (the eye alone indicating the starts) and then intensify the motions up to the sixth note, whose significance is to be underlined every time by a preliminary, emphasizing upbeat, followed by a lightly accenting downbeat.

The definition of a cadence (such as is performed, p. 18, bars 3–4, by the strings *pizzicato*) can be emphasized by sharply-marked impelling motions. These beats are best carried out by the right hand alone, while the left takes charge of the broad continuous melody of the clarinet.

In order to represent the transformation of a motif resulting from a change in its rhythmic constitution, and a new division into one *staccato* half and one *legato* (as on p. 18, bars 6–9), after the first three lightly indicating *staccato* gestures and before the gentle downbeat of bar 8, let the motion linger awhile at the top of the upbeat, and after the downbeat be restricted to marking time and diminution.

Similarly time- and diminution-marking *decrescendo* motions are used in the fourth bar on p. 28. The motion must pause on the third quaver, to end the dying-out phrase. The upbeat at the beginning of the next motif (fourth quaver) thereby gains in strength.

The second and third quavers in bar 1, p. 29, constitute a delay before the final *f* ending of the melody marked 'gemächlich'—*comodo*. Before these two quavers, the melody, *diminuendo*, comes to a lingering, dying-out motion on 'one', after which the motif starts 'schelmisch' (roguishly) on 'two' with a soft impelling motion, to end on 'three' with a similar lingering expiration gesture. This enables us to carry out the actual *f* ending on 'four' with a big upbeat and new impelling motion.

The resources that enable the conductor to impart special intensity to his representation of a work are: the use of the left hand; the use of the eye to govern and watch; and the subdivision of principal motions in order to represent particulars intensively.

Often, indicative 'direction' given to the conducting adequately replaces the eye; e.g. for the three consecutive *ff* entries of the 'celli, and first and second violins, p. 11, bars 3–4. But the Eulenspiegel motif, comically broken up, in the horns (p. 10, last bar, to p. 11, bar 4), has to be brought out by the use of the eye.

'Directed' conducting is especially useful for roving melodic lines, such as begin, p. 39, middle of penultimate bar, in the first and second violins, and are continued in the trumpets (p. 40, bars 1–3), the trombones, and the basses, then again in the trumpets, &c. The eye must be deliberately used, for the first time, on p. 41 for the gathering-up melodic entries of trombones, trumpets, 'celli, and basses.

The eye is particularly useful at places that mark rhythmic articulation or sum up periods—as in the two *ff* entries, in semiquavers, of the woodwind on p. 43. But it also serves to increase the distinctness of harmonic changes (p. 60, last bar but one, the move from A flat to A natural in the 'celli and basses).

We use the left hand, at the very beginning of the work, for a preventative moderating gesture on 'four', before the first 6/8 bar, on p. 3

(*tremolo* of the violins, *pp*), and to secure the *crescendi, crescendi fp*, and *sfz decrescendi* in the first and second violins, pp. 4 and 5.

We represent the simultaneous shades of the *decrescendo* and the *ff* in bar 1, p. 24, by using the two hands to different purposes, the left alone taking charge of the *ff pizzicato* of the double-basses and marking the needful accents.

Subdivisional beats serve to increase the intensity and accuracy of the playing. For the sixth quaver of bar 1, p. 13, we insert an upbeat of the left hand so as to underline the significance of the following downbeat rest, and render the following entry of the woodwind quieter.

In the first two bars of p. 21 we use subdivisional impelling motions of the right hand for the pulses of the timpani in order to ensure that they will take their proper place as complementary articulations between the quavers in the strings and the quavers in the horns.

When players are confronted by exposed and technically difficult passages a little help from the conductor is acceptable. It is advisable for him to take but little notice of difficulties such as, for instance, the beginning of the horn theme (6/8 time on p. 3) affords. All that he has to do at the beginning is to keep an eye on the horn's entry, and then do hardly more than beat the first two bars and a half for the player's benefit. But after this, when the *accelerando* prescribed by the composer starts and until the 'full tempo' ('volles Zeitmass')—that is, for the next three and a half bars—the player must be conducted definitely and helpfully.

It is, perhaps, even more important to be helpful when it is not a single player, but a whole group that has difficulties to face; for instance, p. 16, from bar 4 onwards, the inserted 3/4 bars. Here, as in all similar cases (e.g. the Finale of Schumann's Piano Concerto), avoid accenting and underlining the strong beats—'one' and 'four'—of the bar; but by means of light, small *portato* beats, keep on marking the 6/8 just to give the players their bearings. Any accentuation in the 6/8 quavers will lead the players to respond with hasty mechanical accentuations striving to assert themselves in opposition, and the whole passage will then become inaccurate.

In order to render the course of the music more clearly perceptible, from time to time we conduct rests not with full-size motions, but simply by marking time, until a new entry calls for a return to full motion. This applies to general pause-like breaks such as we encounter on p. 7, last bar, and on p. 8, first bar (on 'one' and 'two').

For the sake of clarity, even alterations such as the following are at times permissible: on p. 32, include the first bar in the pause and start the *tempo primo* with the entry of the orchestra (i.e. the second bar in the score). Thus, without a doubt, the new tempo can be taken more correctly and easily than by keeping to the composer's actual prescriptions.

Lastly, reference should be made to a few habits that prevail in some orchestras and lead to perversions of the composer's intentions.

The *pp* of the *tutti* starting p. 37, last bar, is always made too dense, and the wind play too loud and heavily. The woodwind must be made to 'lighten' their quavers, and the horns, violas, and flutes their answering thirds; very light, elastic motions, hardly more than time-marking, are to be used for this purpose. This brings us up against a bad habit very usual in orchestras: the habit of turning an *espressivo* pure and simple, which is a matter of feeling, into a perceptible increase of intensity and loudness, forgetting that the sweetness of a faintly whispered melody may prove more expressive than a sensuously emphasizing intensification of tone.

A regularly recurring mistake is the wrong accentuation of end-notes— wrong especially at the close of a *decrescendo* such as occurs p. 45, first two and a half bars. No reason can be found for thus 'coming to a full stop'. Let it be precluded, as far as possible, by the use of lessening *decrescendo* motions brought closer and closer to the body, and by beating 'one' in the third bar not by a downbeat, but simply by bringing the right hand close to the body without lowering it, to indicate an expiration.

The same subsiding, lessening *decrescendo* motions are to be used to end the four-bar periods which start p. 66, last bar but two. Unfailingly, the strings and woodwind try to take the rising patterns in semiquavers *crescendo*.

A passage such as the hopping *pizzicato* rhythm on pp. 78 and 79, last three bars, in which the motif-quavers (on 'three', 'four', 'six', and 'one') are always given out too broadly at the expense of accuracy, will

225

be correctly adjusted by the use of very brief *staccato* beats, every one of which is arrested forthwith—beats such as were used in the slow movement of Beethoven's First Symphony to avoid distortion of the rhythm.

In designs played simultaneously and *unisono* by two different orchestral groups, there often is a risk of differences in pace, e.g. in the first two bars of p. 82, when the violins duplicate in *tremolando* semi-quavers the *staccato* motif of the oboes. In the very essence of the *staccato* with its continuous new attacks there lurks a *tempo* heavier than in the quick, volatile *tremolo* of the strings. To prevent the strings from getting even slightly ahead of the oboes, conduct these bars—and, by way of preparation, the foregoing two bars—in calm, stroking, and at the same time checking, and sufficiently ample, *portato* motions.

There is no need to repeat, again and again, how very important it is that the student should be capable of setting a definite basic tempo throughout long stretches and maintaining it in spite of obstacles in his way. In this respect, the first great climax in 'Till Eulenspiegel', up to its apex on the pause, p. 8, affords excellent practice.

The climax that starts p. 40, with the prescription 'immer lebhafter', will teach him how to build up, in one swoop, in one constantly expanding and spreading outburst, a culmination such as is reached, p. 44, bar 5, by the *unisono* call of the horns.

Finally, the Epilogue affords him the opportunity to learn how to impart an even more transparent and graceful character to the tender hues of the first five introductory bars of the work, now repeated without *sfz p* of the woodwind in the second or *crescendo-decrescendo* of the strings in the third. All is changed into a tale of dreamland, into whispering echoes, which only the most subtle, buoyant, indicative gestures can transmute into music.

With 'Till Eulenspiegel' we have dealt with technical problems similar to those we had encountered in Beethoven's First Symphony. With Stravinsky's 'L'Histoire du Soldat', we shall deal with unusual aspects of the pure technique of beating (uneven quintuple and septuple time, &c.). Again we use the pocket score in the Philharmonia edition (no. 294), to which all the indications hereafter will refer.

3. I. STRAVINSKY: 'L'HISTOIRE DU SOLDAT'

In the first section of the third part of this book, 'Conductor and Music', we have dealt with the whole-bar, half-bar, $3/4$, $4/4$, $6/4$, $8/4$, $9/4$, and $12/4$ times—that is those whose periodicity is unambiguous; two of these could be conceived in two different ways:

$\frac{6}{4}$ as $\frac{3}{4}+\frac{3}{4}$ or as $\frac{2}{4}+\frac{2}{4}+\frac{2}{4}$;

$\frac{12}{4}$ as $\frac{3}{4}+\frac{3}{4}+\frac{3}{4}+\frac{3}{4}$ or as $\frac{4}{4}+\frac{4}{4}+\frac{4}{4}$.

But quintuple and septuple time admit of a variety of interpretations, because they consist of both even and odd subdivisions.

$\frac{5}{8}$ can be:

$= \frac{2}{8}+\frac{3}{8}$: p. 7, 3rd and 2nd bars before [3]; p. 9, 5th bar after [10].

$= \frac{3}{8}+\frac{2}{8}$: p. 7, 2nd bar after [4], p. 9, 4th bar after [10].

$= \frac{1}{8}+\frac{2}{8}+\frac{2}{8}$ $(\frac{4}{8})$: p. 25, 3rd bar after [12], bassoon; p. 26, 3rd bar after [15]; p. 61, bar 2; p. 52, 3rd bar after [3].

$= (\frac{4}{8})$ $\frac{2}{8}+\frac{2}{8}+\frac{1}{8}$: p. 49, 2nd bar before [33].

or a whole bar: p. 55, bars 6–8.

Septuple time can be:

$= \frac{2}{8}+\frac{3}{8}+\frac{2}{8}$: p. 9, bar before [11]; p. 47, 3rd bar after [27], and the corresponding bars further.

$\frac{2}{8}+\frac{2}{8}+\frac{3}{8}$: p. 54 [10], and after.

$\frac{4}{16}+\frac{3}{16}$: p. 9, bar before [13].

The representation of these times is achieved not by beating the smallest units (in $5/8$ quavers) but by comprehensive grouping as follows:

$\frac{5}{8}$

$\frac{2}{8}+\frac{3}{8}=$ $\frac{3}{8}+\frac{2}{8}=$

$\frac{1}{8}+\frac{2}{8}+\frac{2}{8}\langle\frac{4}{8}\rangle=$ $\langle\frac{4}{8}\rangle\frac{2}{8}+\frac{2}{8}+\frac{1}{8}=$

$\frac{7}{8}$

$\frac{2}{8}+\frac{3}{8}+\frac{2}{8}=$ $\frac{2}{8}+\frac{2}{8}+\frac{3}{8}=$ $\frac{4}{16}+\frac{3}{16}=$

227

The essence of metre consists in the fact that an invariable, very small value (be it quaver, crotchet, or minim) is the unit of measurement, whereas rhythm consists in the allocation into periods, grouping, and combination of such units into patterns.

The peculiar and, at first sight, bewildering idiosyncrasy of Stravinsky's music is the introduction, over the basic metre, of the most various rhythms, often in conflict with the primary metric schemes (2/8, 3/8, 4/8, &c.). This is something unknown to both classical and modern music, and therefore a special style of representation is needful. Before tackling the matter, let us show by a few examples how, in 'L'Histoire du Soldat', such contrasts between metre and rhythm occur.

(1) Changing rhythms *versus* invariable metre.

The metre may occur in its simplest form, as in the motif-like bar-group in the *basso ostinato* from [1] on p. 1: 'Marche du Soldat'.

First the metric bar-group (2/4) is contrasted with a superimposed 3/4 pattern (p. 2, bar 1). The result is that when this pattern falls upon the next 2/4 bar (p. 2, bar 2), its gravity is distributed in the opposite way. And the following two 3/8 bars seem to deny, absolutely, the natural accent-values of the 2/4 (these values coinciding in turn with the first, third, and second quavers). We have the combinations:

A peculiarity is that none of the new rhythmic groups is divisible. This, it is true, is no longer the case in the third bar after [3], p. 2, where the 3/8 consists of ⌐♩♩♩, or 1/8+1/4 (the bar before [4] is similarly constituted). In the second bar after [7], p. 3, we have ⌐ ⌐ ♫, and in bar [10] p. 5, ⌐♩, both of which equal 1/8+1/4.

228

Similar cases are:

The beginning of 'The King's March', p. 19, where 5/8 occurs over a concealed 2/4 metre:

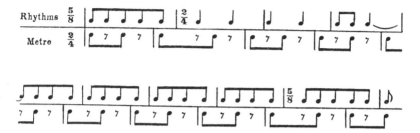

Bar [1] on p. 7 of 'Music by the Stream', where 3/8 and 4/8 collide:

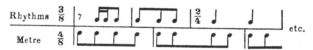

The third bar before [3] on p. 7, with 5/8 over 4/8:

The third bar after [13], p. 9:

Bar 7 on p. 31:

229

(2) Changing rhythms over several different but simultaneous metres: Bar [21] on p. 35.

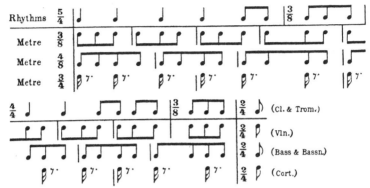

In the above examples rhythm and metre, opposed to one another, co-operate in building form; but instead of metre we may have a substitute. All manifestations of metre, so far, were due to motif-like groups; and therefore, we may have, instead of the constant metre, similar group-formations in succession to represent the metre. This occurs with *ostinato*, rhythmic motifs, symmetrically organized and sustained time-values, and combinations of distinguishable metre-parts in succession.

(3) Changing rhythms versus *ostinato* patterns.

We find such *ostinato* patterns in lieu of metre, under rich and variously articulated rhythms in the runs in sixths of the violins from the third bar before [7], p. 8, onwards. It is characteristic that this combination of rhythm and *ostinato* appears more soft and supple than that of rhythm and metre.

(4) Changing rhythms *versus* rhythmic motifs.

In the 'Tango' (p. 39), the percussion motif 3/4 ⌐• ♪♪♪⌐ is opposed to the melody of the violins, providing articulation. It begins now on one beat of the bar, now on another; on 'three' in the first bar, on 'one' in the fourth, on 'four' in the second after [1]. Every time its beginning must be accented (indicated).

The same principle is illustrated, in a more complicated form, in 'The King's March', p. 28. On the fourth quaver of the second bar after [18], a motif consisting of three quavers and given out by bass and violins, ♩ ♫♩, appears and is heard three times successively.

(5) Changing rhythms *versus* symmetrically organized sustained time values.

In the 'Music by the Stream' at [9] we have the following:

(6) Different rhythms *versus* combinations of distinguishable metre-parts in succession.

In the 'Tango', p. 40, at [4], we have the following: firstly the rhythmic pattern ♪♪♪ ♪; then, four bars farther, the same without the rest ♪♪♪; after the end of the fifth bar, again ♪♪♪ ♪; and in bars 6–7, by way of ending, again ♪♪♪:

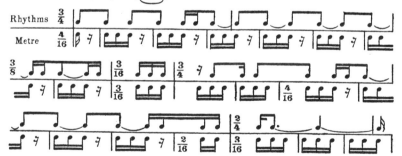

In the next example we have the succession of 3/8 and 4/8, each with a different motif:

231

(7) A last, and indeed an extreme, case of other factors replacing the simple metric group-patterns is the combination of several rhythms, equal in value to one another, but entirely different, as occur simultaneously at the beginning of the 'Little Concert' (p. 30) in the three parts. These three rhythms are but superficially interconnected by their common smallest unit, the quaver.

In view of representing this complicated music, observe the following points:

(1) Bars in which a contrasting rhythm is introduced over an unvarying metre, without any division being possible, are to be beaten simply, on the basis of the smallest metric value in them. Thus in the second bar before [3], p. 2, and bar [1], p. 7, it is important to avoid underlining, by an accenting downbeat, the entry of a contrasting rhythm, but it must be taken in light, time-marking motions, as though carrying on without change. The best way, at the start of a change of rhythm, is, instead of carrying the downbeat on 'one' to its normal nethermost point, to measure out time indicatively, down to half length, and then to continue in a sideways curve, reverting to the normal length of downbeat only when the basic metre finally reappears.

By way of example, here is the beating for the first five bars of p. 2. The first four are to be taken lightly, just marking time, and only the fifth (at [3]) is taken in normal motions:

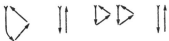

If care is not taken to resort, in such cases, to non-accenting, decreased downbeats, performance will be marred by displacements and inaccuracies, the ensemble will start tottering; the players giving out the various consecutive rhythms (here the cornet and the trombone) will break up the general *melos* by introducing accents, and the double-bass marking the general metre will, when there is a shifting (as in the bar before [3]), involuntarily respond to the emphasizing downbeat with a false after-beat accentuation.

As with this simple case, so with compound time. For instance, in the 5/8, p. 7, third bar before [3], the articulation 2/8 + 3/8 must not be marked by a second downbeat on 'three'. The best way is to conduct as follows:

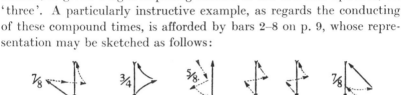

Thus the third quaver, given an accent in both bars by the composer himself, is given a light impelling motion to the left and upwards, on 'three'. A particularly instructive example, as regards the conducting of these compound times, is afforded by bars 2–8 on p. 9, whose representation may be sketched as follows:

(2) Bars in which a contrasting rhythm comes over an unvarying metre, but in which there is a period-division, are not beaten on the basis of the smallest metric value in them, but their structure is represented.

For instance, in the third bar after [3], p. 2, the 3/8 consists of one quaver-value which belongs, so to speak, to the foregoing pattern, forming its conclusion, and of a crotchet-value which is definitely an upbeat, the anacrusis of the pattern in the next 3/4 bar: It is most important, therefore, to give the downbeat on 'one' of the 3/8 bar a merely indicative, time-marking character, and to accent and 'push' the upbeat on 'two, three'. As the space available for this upbeat has been decreased by the shortening of the downbeat on 'one', the impelling motion must be carried out, at first away from the body, forwards, and then upwards.

The same applies to the bar before [4], p. 2, although this bar seems to be similar to the bar after [3]; and the same principle again applies to the second bar after [7], p. 3, although there is no period-division in it: for then, it becomes possible for the clarinet to give out, quietly and without 'tottering', the next 2/4 bar into which its two upbeat-semiquavers must lead, as the second half of a regular crotchet-upbeat

Another corresponding case occurs at [18], p. 28. Here, on the second quaver, all the instruments start the equivalent of the bassoon melody appearing on p. 27, second bar after [17], but without the trombone, which, ending its run, makes to return to its starting-point B flat. This amalgamation of end and starting-point has the result of shifting the entry of the melody on to the weak beat of the bar, making it come in one crotchet sooner, and in the form of an accented upbeat: hence, the passage is to be conducted as the previous examples.

These explanations will have clearly shown the student how to deal with longer melodic patterns in which the two orders of cases so far considered are mingled—as, e.g. on p. 13, from [10] to [13]. This brings us to the last point that need concern us. In music such as Stravinsky's in 'L'Histoire du Soldat', the main thing is clearly to realize the contrasting combinations of metre and rhythm; and the decisive factor will be the correct technical use of impelling motions and simple time-marking. A skilful use of both processes is specially important as regards:

1. *Coincidences of endings and starting-points.*

A particularly illuminating example occurs p. 20, bars 2–5. In both 5/8 bars the end of a phrase and the beginning of another coincide. Therefore, it is not enough to use the method of conducting previously learned—

for then we should lack an upbeat-break for 'three'. The downbeat on 'one' must be almost arrested midway, and rise, barely perceptibly, for the second quaver; thereby it becomes possible to use a second, slight downbeat for 'three'.

2. *Direct succession (without a rest) of ending and beginning.*

This occurs p. 22, bars 5–6. It is advisable to conduct the 3/8 bar before [7] so as to lead on, with decreasing downward motion, to 'one' of bar 7, which should not be accented.

But it is needful that the whole downward course of the motions in this 3/8 should not exceed half the length of a normal downbeat, so that the next downbeat at [7] should take place unaccented, from top to bottom of the other half-length.

3. *Interrupting, inserted bars between end and start.*

The bar before [21], p. 35, is in 5/8 time and stands as a 'veto' staving off a direct continuation of what has occurred so far. For this reason, and also because of the stipulated accent and *forte*, its entry must be emphasized and accented. The previous two bars ($\frac{3}{8}+\frac{1}{4}$) are merely the *diminuendo* ending of the melody started at [20] by the clarinet. In order to represent this fact, and also to gain the high starting-point needed for the full-strength f downbeat that has to follow, the last four bars before [21] should be conducted more or less thus:

(That is, the final 1/4 bar is represented by a whole-bar beat taken *p staccato*). As for the 5/8 bar, it must be taken in decreasing motions, the recommencement of the clarinet melody at [21] being at the same time prepared. The best way is to divide it, more or less, into 2/8+3/8, which subside into one another:

Most helpful is the lingering upbeat motion, which is to be used whenever (as on p. 35, bars 2, 4, and 5 after [20]) decreasing, terminating appendices follow a one-bar melodic 'head'. This gesture raises the third crotchet-beat upbeatwise, over the starting-point of motion, and with the 3/8 is carried back lightly, to the normal height, from which the second 3/4 bar may be started normally.

The importance of the technique by means of which period-divisions can be clearly articulated is clearly shown by what occurs from [27] to the end of p. 47. The combinations

$$\tfrac{4}{8}+\tfrac{3}{16}+\tfrac{7}{16}; \ \tfrac{4}{8}+\tfrac{5}{16}+\tfrac{7}{16}; \ \tfrac{4}{8}+\tfrac{5}{16}+\tfrac{7}{16}; \ \tfrac{4}{8}+\tfrac{5}{16}+\tfrac{7}{16}; \ \tfrac{4}{8}+\tfrac{3}{16}+\tfrac{7}{16}; \ \tfrac{2}{8}+\tfrac{5}{16}$$

are to be represented by a compound $\frac{2}{16}+\frac{3}{16}$ metre, both parts of which, according to their duration, are taken in beats of various length:

Two particularly difficult passages call for special explanations.

(1) P. 24 at [11], to p. 25, third bar after [13].

With the third quaver of the bar marked [11], the cornet starts a melodic curve which at bar 1, p. 25, passes on to the bassoon, to be continued when the cornet enters again (upbeat before [12], p. 25), reverting to the bassoon (second bar after [12]), and being ended by the cornet.

The difficulty, here, lies in the fact that it is impossible to give much attention to an effortless performance of the 2/4 metre ; it is so vital that the melodic line should be clearly represented by the conductor, that every other consideration remains subordinate. It is only by accurately keeping to the smallest metric unit, the quaver, that the conductor can help, in turn, the trombone and the clarinet, the bass and the violin, the bassoon and again the clarinet. But at [11] we have, firstly, a possibly misleading accent on the third quaver; the same thing occurs in the second bar before [12], and in the third after [12] we have two new irritating melodic accents. It is advisable, in order to facilitate the performance of the fourth bar before [12] (p. 25), to divide the 3/8 into ♪ + ♫ ; that is, into a terminating quaver belonging to the pattern in the previous bar and a crotchet-upbeat very accurately beginning the next phrase. The third bar, 5/8, after [12] is to be conducted thus:

differentiating ♪ + ♫ + ♫

There remains to consider whether the second bar, 3/8, after [13] should not be divided into ╕ + ╕ ♬ , because only thereby (as was the case with the second bar after [7], p. 3) can the clarinet enter and pass on to the next bar, 2/8, without effort or danger of 'tottering'.

(2) P. 52, from third bar before [3], to p. 53, bar 4.

If we compare the metre and the rhythms, the special difficulty of this passage will become evident:

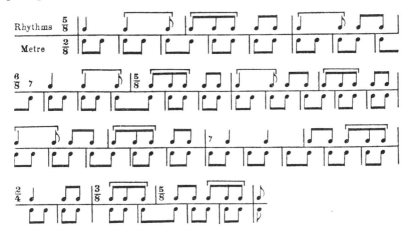

In order to represent these diverse rhythms, we again resort to the compound metre 2/8+3/8, which crops up in the following six combinations, with various lengths of beat according to the different durations of 2/8 and 3/8 respectively:

237

1. $\frac{5}{8}$ ♩   +   ♩ ♪   = $\frac{2}{8} + \frac{3}{8}$

2. $\frac{5}{8}$ ♫ + ♫♪   = $\frac{2}{8} + \frac{3}{8}$

3. $\frac{5}{8}$ ♩ ♪ + ♫   = $\frac{3}{8} + \frac{2}{8}$

4. $\frac{5}{8}$ ♫♪ + ♫   = $\frac{3}{8} + \frac{2}{8}$

5. $\frac{5}{8}$ ♪ + ♩   +   ♩   = $\frac{1}{8} + \frac{2}{8} + \frac{2}{8}$

6. $\frac{6}{8}$ ♪ + ♩   +   ♩ ♪   = $\frac{1}{8} + \frac{2}{8} + \frac{3}{8}$

Apart from the absolute need to keep most accurately and with the utmost care to the smallest metric unit, the quaver, which must remain absolutely invariable, there is the additional difficulty that the changing rhythms occur, parallel and simultaneous, in two or even three voices. Therefore, they must be represented very illuminatingly and unambiguously. The usual way of beating the first three bars—

may be improved by marking faint quaver-subdivisions, following the melodic progress, on the fifth quaver of the first bar and on the third of the second and third bars:

Similar subdivisions will represent the period-division of the fourth and tenth bars (6/8 and 5/8 respectively):

Bar 4, $\frac{6}{8}$ =

Bar 10, $\frac{5}{8}$ =

The student should now be able to achieve an unimpeachable representation of 'L'Histoire du Soldat'. The only requirements are that after thoroughly studying the problems in the work, he should apply all that he has learned, and that he should never forget the following points:

(1) In all combinations, the smallest metric unit (♪ in: ♩; ♩ ♪; ♪ ♩; ♫♫, &c.—no matter how many motions go to beating it) must be kept invariable.

(2) He must avoid needless accents in changes of rhythm, thereby not rendering it more difficult to count out the smallest metric values quickly.

(3) He must not forget to characterize and represent, discreetly but with thorough clarity, all coincidences of beginnings and endings.

(4) He must never be misled into hurrying or prolonging, however slightly it be, irregular end- or upbeat-values (e.g. in the 'Tango', p. 40, fourth bar after [4], whose expiring 3/16 must be represented by a quiet quaver-beat, extended over the duration of the 3/16; and in 'The Devil's Triumphal March', bar before [9], when the three upbeat semiquavers, which tend to hurry on, must also be taken in a quiet quaver-beat, exactly corresponding to the 3/16.

In the library of one of the big theatres in Germany there is an orchestral part upon which an observant and intelligent player wrote the following note (with reference to the well-known beginning: *Allegro,*

3/8 (♩.); | ♩. ♪ ♫ | ♪ | : 'Mr. A. beats this bar thus':

∪

(that is, without preliminary upbeat, in exact accord with the music). 'Mr. B. gives an upbeat':

∪ ∪

(this upbeat is unnecessary, but may do no harm if performed by the left hand, indicatively, while the right stands poised, ready for the down-beat, to start as Mr. A. is said to start).

'Mr. C. tells the orchestra that he will give two preparatory metro-nomic beats to mark the time before the first bar of the music' (quite unnecessary)—'he therefore imperatively requires a rehearsal.'

239

'As regards Mr. D. it can only be said that in his case each player must find out for himself what use his conducting is; anyway, nothing ever goes together under him.'

This anecdote mercilessly exposes the weakest point of conducting as commonly practised. For every technical problem there is one solution; an intelligible, unequivocal one which any orchestral player will understand without having rehearsed and without preliminary explanations. This art of conducting unambiguously is our only goal, and the one thing we insist upon from all conductors.

An instrument, be it violin or pianoforte, can only give out what is played on it; but an orchestral player gives out that which in his opinion is what the conductor is aiming at. Therefore, ambiguity means unsatisfactory results, and a wide range of possible misapprehensions. The first and foremost duty of the conductor is to be capable of always avoiding ambiguity in representation, so as to ensure flawless, unambiguous renderings.

The third part of this book attempts to show a rational and practicable way of achieving this. The second part has acquainted the student with the weaknesses and obstacles which result either from the nature of the instruments or from the way in which they are played. It is only when a conductor has acquired perfect mastery over this province of his duties that his work at rehearsals will not only lead the players to study the works they have to play, but ensure a permanent improvement in the standard of performance.

But the first and foremost conditions of good work in conducting were dealt with in the first part, which set forth the kind of musicianship, of artistic and general education by virtue of which a musician can qualify for becoming a conductor. It was pointed out, repeatedly, that the main requirement was a capacity to form, in advance, carefully studied ideal conceptions of the works to be played—mental models of the actual results to be aimed at. During the tuition the teacher should have proved capable of showing the student the various ways in which an orchestra reacts, and of teaching him how to deal with the weak points in the players and the playing; how to anticipate and prevent, improve and intensify, and smooth difficulties. If so, the student, when facing an orchestra for the first time, will be capable of doing the very best that

240

can be wished for: of ensuring, without preliminary rehearsal or mutual acquaintanceship, technically flawless and musically unimpeachable performance.

This should not be considered as a result out of the common, when one remembers how very much is expected from any solo-player or singer who makes his first public appearance. And yet, until now, it seemed altogether Utopian, and nobody ever dared expect it from a conductor known to be facing, really for the first time, the particular instrument which is the orchestra.

MODERN WORKS

FROM WHICH EXAMPLES ARE GIVEN

BERG, ALBAN: Kammerkonzert for piano and violin. Vienna, Universal Edition.

BRUCKNER, ANTON:

    II. Symphony. Vienna, Ludwig Doblinger.

    III. Symphony, D-moll. Vienna, A. Bösendorfers.

    VIII. Symphony. Vienna, Carl Haslinger.

    IX. Symphony. Vienna, Ludwig Doblinger.

BUSONI, FERRUCCIO: Turandot. Leipzig, Breitkopf & Härtel.

CASELLA, ALFREDO: Op. 11. Italia. Vienna, Universal Edition.

HINDEMITH, PAUL:

    Kammermusik Nr. 1

    Piano Concerto

    Orchestra Concerto   } Mainz, B. Schott's Söhne.

    Violin Concerto

HONEGGER, ARTHUR: Pacific 231. Paris, M. Senart.

KAMINSKI, HEINRICH: Concerto Grosso for 2 orchestras. Magnificat. Vienna, Universal Edition.

LENDVAI, ERWIN: Kammersuite I. Hamburg, Benjamin.

MAHLER, GUSTAV:

    II. Symphony

    III. Symphony   } Vienna, Josef Weinberger.

    V. Symphony. Leipzig, C. F. Peters.

    VIII. Symphony

    IX. Symphony   } Vienna–Leipzig, Universal Edition.

    Das Lied von der Erde

MIASKOWSKI, NIKOLAI: VII. Symphony. Vienna, Universal Edition.

REGER, MAX:

    Serenade. Berlin, Bote & Bock.

    Sinfonietta. Leipzig, Lauterbach.

    Symphonic Prologue. Leipzig, C. F. Peters.

242

SCHÖNBERG, ARNOLD:
  Chamber Symphony. Vienna, Universal Edition.
  Op. 16. 5 Orchestral pieces. Leipzig, C. F. Peters.
  Verklärte Nacht. Berlin, Verlag Dreililien.

STRAUSS, RICHARD:
  Don Juan
  Till Eulenspiegel } Vienna, Universal Edition.

STRAVINSKY, IGOR:
  L'Histoire du Soldat
  Les Noces } London, J. W. Chester, Ltd.
  Suite de Pulcinella. Berlin, Russ. Musikverlag.
  I. Suite for small orchestra
  II. Suite for small orchestra } London, J. W. Chester, Ltd.

TIESSEN, HEINZ: Prologue to a Drama of Revolution. Berlin, Ries & Erler.

TOCH, ERNST: Op. 39. Piano Concerto. Mainz, B. Schott's Söhne.

WEBERN, ANTON:
  Op. 6
  Op. 10 } Vienna, Universal Edition.